Human Sexuality and the Nuptial Mystery

HUMAN SEXUALITY
and the
Nuptial Mystery

EDITED BY
ROY R. JEAL

CASCADE *Books* • Eugene, Oregon

HUMAN SEXUALITY AND THE NUPTIAL MYSTERY

Copyright © 2010 Wipf and Stock Publishers. All rights reserved. Except for brief quotations in critical publications or reviews, no part of this book may be reproduced in any manner without prior written permission from the publisher. Write: Permissions, Wipf and Stock Publishers, 199 W. 8th Ave., Suite 3, Eugene, OR 97401.

Cascade Books
An Imprint of Wipf and Stock Publishers
199 W. 8th Ave., Suite 3
Eugene, OR 97401

www.wipfandstock.com

"Being Born is Important" from BREATHING TOKENS by Carl Sandburg, copyright © 1978 by Maurice C. Greenbaum and Frank M. Parker, Trustees of the Sandburg Family Trust and Harcourt, Inc., reprinted by permission of Houghton Mifflin Harcourt Publishing Company.

ISBN 13: 978-1-60608-944-6

Cataloging-in-Publication data:

Human sexuality and the nuptial mystery / edited by Roy R. Jeal ; foreword by David Widdicombe and Kirsten Pinto Gfroerer.

xx + 164 p. ; 23 cm.

ISBN 13: 978-1-60608-944-6

1. Human body—Religious aspects. 2. Anglican Communion—Doctrines. 3. Homosexuality—Religious aspects—Anglican Communion. I. Jeal, Roy R. II. Widdicombe, David. III. Gfroerer, Kirsten Pinto.

BR115. H6 H85 2010

Manufactured in the U.S.A.

Contents

List of Contributors | vii

Foreword by David Widdicombe and Kirsten Pinto Gfroerer | ix

Preface by Roy R. Jeal | xiii

Précis by Preston Parsons | xix

On the Nature of Desire: A Sermon on Ecclesiastes 12:1–8 and Proverbs 13:12 | 1
John Stafford

Desire, Vocation, and Friendship: The Mysteries of Human Sexuality

1 How Can We Frame the Right Questions? | 9
  Oliver O'Donovan

2 Ideology, Argumentation, and Social Direction in Romans 1 | 27
  Roy R. Jeal

3 Friendship: The End of Marriage | 45
  Gary Thorne

4 Bodies without Borders: Desire, Abjection, and Human Sexuality in Recent Theology | 65
  Jane Barter Moulaison

The Nuptial Mystery: The Sacrament of Marriage

5 The Nuptial Mystery: The Historical Flesh of Procreation | 85
  Ephraim Radner

6 Visions of Marriage in Ephesians 5 | 116
  Roy R. Jeal

7   Becoming One: The Christian Story and the Politics
    of Marriage | 131
    Christopher R. J. Holmes

8   Forbid Them Not: The Place of Children in a Theology
    of Marriage | 148
    Tim Perry

Contributors

Christopher R. J. Holmes is Associate Professor of Systematic Theology and Ethics at Providence Seminary, Otterburne, Manitoba

Roy R. Jeal is Professor of Religion at Booth College and Scholar in Residence at St. Margaret's Anglican Church, Winnipeg

Jane Barter Moulaison is Associate Professor of Church History in the Faculty of Theology at the University of Winnipeg

Oliver O'Donovan is Professor of Christian Ethics and Practical Theology in the School of Divinity, New College, University of Edinburgh

Preston Parsons is Rector of St. Mary Magdalene Anglican Church, Winnipeg

Tim Perry is Associate Professor of Theology at Providence College, Otterburne, Manitoba

Ephraim Radner is Professor of Historical Theology at Wycliffe College, University of Toronto

John Stafford is Dean of Theology in St. John's College at the University of Manitoba

Gary Thorne is Chaplain at King's College, Dalhousie University and a member of the Primate's Theological Commission

Foreword

At its General Synod held in June 2007, bishops of the Anglican Church of Canada asked for more time to study the theology surrounding the blessing of same-sex unions. The Parish of St. Margaret's decided to try its hand at what the bishops seemed to be asking for. The vision was to renew theological discussions of the sacrament of marriage and human sexuality by hosting a consultation for bishops, clergy, theologians, lay people, and, particularly, young people on this topic and to do our theological work hemmed in by the worship of the church.

The reader might wonder why a small, ordinary Anglican parish in Canada should take the trouble to do this. The topic is obvious enough, but the idea to hold a parish-based theological consultation on such a difficult and divisive issue might seem incautious. But undertake such a conference the parish did—the first of, we hope, many on various topics. For while we were glad to imagine that we might be able to make some contribution to this debate, we had a broader agenda in mind, namely, to make a modest contribution to a creative, parish-based theological renewal of the evangelical/catholic center in Anglicanism. A brief word about our aims might help to clarify this ambition and provide a context for the essays that follow.

First, it was our intent to concentrate on depth rather than breadth. As a parish we are not convinced that there are only two options in this debate. We wanted to explore the classical or orthodox centre of Christian thought on the subject of human sexuality with enough rigor to discover how many creative dimensions, alternatives, problems, or subsidiary matters might emerge from within this perspective on its own terms. Believing, as we do, that there are no topics of concern to the people called Christian that do not belong within an ordered account of Church doctrine, we assumed that the immensely important subject of human sexuality must surely be as good a way as any into the joyful science of theology. Over the long haul, where there is enough patience and good will, the thinking through of any issue in obedience to Jesus Christ can only help the Church to discover its catholic unity in the gospel. Even if no immediately practical ways forward emerge, intractable problems also yield their own theological rewards when we attempt to understand more exactly what it is that makes them intractable. The practical reasonableness required for those integrity-preserving agreements the Church must have if it is to do its work of moral and political education in the world stems in part from its ability to name what it finds to be irresolvable and why. It is not a bad thing, surely, for the Church to struggle with truths it can neither fully comprehend in theory nor entirely reconcile in practice. A failure to agree in holy investigation is not always reason for despair when the work has been done well.

Second, we wanted to plant the idea of theological/liturgical consultations that would help bridge the gap between the Church and the Academy, *from the side of the Church*. Christ is learned when we encounter him in the sacred texts and at the table. The site of theology is Eucharistic and Christ himself is the theologian, the Bishop is his delegate, and the theologian the Bishop's. It is a good thing, surely, when any parish church invites its theologians to sit with their Bishop and to expound the saving texts in church to church people while in the midst of their liturgy. Perhaps parishes should do this more often. As Jean-Luc Marion has written, "theology cannot aim at any other progress than its own conversion to the Word, the theologian again becoming bishop or else one of the poor believers, in the common Eucharist."[1]

In one sense, the topic of our consultation did not matter except insofar as it gave the participants an opportunity to think long and hard about a topic that relates deeply to our human condition as we stand before God, and to do so in the context of worship. The intention was to let this topic open on the whole scope of Christian doctrine and to situate it in the lived liturgical experience of a Church that thinks its prayers and prays its thinking. Even topics as vexed and complex as human sexuality, marriage, celibacy, and procreation can lead us deeper into the joy of believing. As Marion puts it, in theology we are free because all is already "given, gained, available."[2]

---

1. Jean-Luc Marion, *God Without Being*, trans. Thomas A. Carlson (Chicago and London: University of Chicago Press, 1991) 158.

2. Ibid.

There are many people to whom thanks is due for making this consultation possible. We thank the Bishop of Rupert's Land, the Rt. Rev. Donald Philips, who made financial resources available and warmly welcomed participants into his Diocese. We thank all the bishops who attended, particularly Bishop Victoria Matthews and members of the Primate's Theological Commission. We owe a special debt of gratitude to the Anglican Foundation for their financial support, and to the parishioners who sponsored many of the student and young adult members of the consultation. Thanks go to Don Betts, who managed the consultation, and to Christina Holmes and Donna Royer and their many volunteers, for their administrative support. We acknowledge the sustaining moral and financial support of the Wardens, Vestry, and people of St. Margaret's. Our debt to Ruth Widdicombe, the Parish Liturgist and Music Director, was obvious to all who attended worship.

Finally, thank you to each person whose essay is included in this volume, especially to Dr. Roy Jeal, our Scholar in Residence, who has undertaken the time-consuming task of editing this collection. We commend his fine Introduction to readers. Finally, we must express our deep appreciation to Professors Oliver O'Donovan and Ephraim Radner, our keynote speakers, whose gracious participation, wise counsel, and formidable scholarship made the dream a reality.

David Widdicombe, Rector
Kirsten Pinto Gfroerer, Conference Planner

Preface

The essays in this book were presented at the St. Margaret's Consultation on Doctrine Liturgy and Preaching held at St. Margaret's Anglican Church in Winnipeg, Canada, in April 2008. The aim of the Consultation was to look for creative alternatives to the polarization of the ongoing debates about human sexuality and marriage, and to do so from a theological rather than polemical standpoint, since it is theology that shapes Christian discourse. The essays explore tensions and imaginative options regarding sexuality and marriage within the classical Christian tradition. The Consultation made suggestions in important and helpful ways, rather than drawing final conclusions about the issues. The need for such consultation is evident because our understanding of the gospel, Scripture, Christian faith and behavior must be studied, discussed, and learned in every generation. These essays demonstrate the creativity that Preston Parsons refers to in his Précis as "playing on the field of Scripture, investigating and interrogating our traditions of interpretation" and that this "playing" can be done without being sidelined by antagonism or resentment. Certainly the topics discussed arouse passions that make for distant and isolating polarities. They are at once very personal yet theological and social matters that touch on beliefs, souls, behaviors, families, and communities. There is no easy agreement, and division seems always to be a threatening presence on the horizon. These essays, however, propose thoughtful and hopeful, and, at times, controversial, dialogue.

The consultation was founded on specific principles:
- The Evangelical Principle: Jesus Christ as attested by the prophets and apostles of the Holy Scriptures and as present in his resurrected body, is the source of our hope, the ground of our obedience, and the center of our thinking;

- The Catholic Principle: led by the Holy Spirit, the Church is one in unity, holy in proclamation and obedience, catholic in universality and diversity, and apostolic in faith and doctrine. The Church must seek to exemplify each of these marks in their fullness;
- The Parish Principle: theology speaks from the pulpit and the table; it is rooted in worship. The intellectual vigor of the church cannot surpass the quality of theological commitment in parish liturgy and proclamation.

This volume begins with a Précis that sets the stage with brief commentary about the idea, value, and hope of such a Consultation and with John Stafford's sermon, "On the Nature of Desire," that starts the discussion with a theological, pastoral, and implicitly gospel-focused reflection on the task at hand, and of the difficulty we have, being humans with desires of many kinds, yet who are inevitably confronted with the fading of desire, with fear, and the prospect of death. The body of the book is set out in two sections. The first, "Desire, Vocation and Friendship: The Mysteries of Human Sexuality," explores biblical, theological, and ethical issues surrounding human sexuality and considers relationships in these particular Christian contexts. The second section, "The Nuptial Mystery: The Sacrament of Marriage," explores the biblical, spiritual, and procreative nature and force of marriage and family.

In his keynote presentation, "How Can We Frame the Right Questions?," Oliver O'Donovan states that "Before we can talk about the meeting of the sexes, before we can talk of the experience of being sexed, we must recognize the *being* of the sexes." O'Donovan takes up Mark D. Jordan's book, *The Ethics of Sex*, as an example of a work that offers a clear position regarding same-sex relations stated by gay believers who practice prayer and discipleship. For dialogue to occur, it is important to hear what gay believers themselves say, not only what others say about them. O'Donovan also refers to the *St. Andrew's Day Statement*, which seeks to elicit dialogue with and promote listening to gay Christians in order for all sides to learn about others' views. The article proceeds to set out five crucial and critical questions addressed to gay Christians as a serious call for dialogue and careful listening, aiming to clarify their relation to historical and accepted Christian understandings. This straightforward and thoughtful approach is necessary in order to avoid the atmosphere of incrimination that surrounds discussion and is typically used to evade and disclaim responsibility, to blame others, and inhibits finding answers to pressing issues.

Roy Jeal, in "Ideology, Argumentation and Social Direction in Romans 1," considers the central New Testament text relevant to Church discussions about homoerotic behavior and same sex relationships. Paul's ideology and argumentation in the letter aim to shape the church in particular ways that accord with the gospel. In Rom 1:26–27, as part of a larger argument in Romans 1–3, Paul argues that same-sex intercourse is not in accord with how humans should honor God. He does not claim that homosexual behavior is more egregious than anything else, nor does he claim that some behaviors incur more or stronger consequences than others. His larger argument indicates that *all of us* stand guilty before God. No one is better than anyone else, Jew or Gentile, gay or straight, and we may not disparage or hate anyone or fail to respect anyone. Still, Paul does not validate homosexual activity. The point for Paul was not about freedom to do things, but doing things so that proclamation of Christ could be made for the sake of the salvation of others.

The essay "Friendship: The End of Marriage" by Gary Thorne addresses the debate in the Anglican Church about performing wedding ceremonies for same-sex couples or blessing the weddings of same-sex couples performed by civil authorities. Thorne suggests that same-sex relationships should be understood by Christians in the context of friendship, which is necessary to becoming fully human and is the means by which Christians grow in virtue, moral character, and holiness. He takes up the ideas of Pavel Florensky to describe the nature of such friendship. There is an ancient Christian tradition of a "covenanted friendship" of persons of the same sex that has been blessed, offered to God in prayer, and involves living together in sacrificial sharing. This tradition was largely lost or set aside at the time of the Reformation. Such friendships, however, express *philia*, *agapē*, and even *eros*. Calling these friendships "marriage" is mistaken, and would end or destroy Christian marriage.

Jane Barter Moulaison, in "Bodies without Borders: Desire, Abjection and Human Sexuality in Recent Theology," describes how humans inhabit a world ("cities") where sexual desire is promised as a fulfillment that never occurs, and where only frustration is actually produced. The fulfillment of desire is an unattainable ideal and the real has become abject, rejected. Bodies have become the consumables of desire that are abandoned and despised after use rather than honored and served. In the Church, however, desire is to be seen as corrected, where it involves care for the abandoned, the unbeautiful, the despised, and the abject. Barter Moulaison argues that in the Church homosexuals (and others, often women) must be become our friends precisely because they have suffered abjection. Christ himself was despised and rejected and we are called to be followers of the abjected Messiah and to serve those who have been seen as undesirable. We must not impose or maintain abjection on others. Friendship is a characteristic of a community that understands hope and has a view toward the eventual grand banquet of those made full in Christ.

Ephraim Radner, in his keynote presentation "The Nuptial Mystery: The Historical Flesh of Procreation," claims that the "mystery" of marriage in the Bible and in the Church is "procreative—generative in a child-producing way," that marriage and children simply go together. While recognizing the difficulties of his claim, Radner states that marriage is not in the first instance about desire or self-worth or relationship with another or about God, but about children. Husband and wife leave their first family to become the roots of a new family. The joining of things together is fundamentally procreative. Marriage is an *analogia creationis*, an analogy to creation that is meant to give life. The mystery of marriage is grounded in this givenness of the life-bearing vocation of bodies. Human bodies are life-bearers and are to pass life along to new life and nurture it toward fullness.

In "Visions of Marriage in Ephesians 5," Roy Jeal examines and interprets the biblical text that explicitly mentions and describes the "great mystery" of marriage. Visualization of the images of marriage presented, of men, women, bodies, Christ, and Church, enables readers to be drawn into the world of the text. The apocalyptic picturing shows what Christ has done for the Church by giving himself for it and, similarly, how husbands and wives give themselves up for the sake of the other. Wives and husbands are called to order their bodily lives in accord with what Christ has done for the Church so that the Church will be what it is, a glorious, apocalyptically shaped body. The great nuptial mystery is that marriage is for the good of the other person. God blesses the Church with fullness, salvation, and dignity for all in it. Ephesians 5 calls for believers to grasp and physically embody this mystery, particularly in marriage.

Christopher Holmes, in his essay "Becoming One: The Christian Story and the Politics of Marriage," asks "What *is* marriage?" and "What is the *purpose* of marriage?" His questions are important because, he indicates, marriage has become "domesticated" as something that we humans control for our own reasons and benefits, with redemption and God being afterthoughts rather than being at the forefront. He shows that the frame of reference for marriage must not be the way of the world, but its origin in God and in God's reconciling actions. Marriage is not in the first instance about humans and their needs or desires, but about God and his salvific work in Christ. Marriage is an indicator of God's love and call to faithfulness. It is a demonstration to the world of the love of God and of neighbor.

In "Forbid Them Not: The Place of Children in a Theology of Marriage," Tim Perry points out that children have become so objectified in Western culture that they are not so much human beings as objects of desire. They have become consumer items. What is often missing in Christian discussion is the place of children in "a theologically robust account of marriage." Perry argues that "our understanding of marriage will remain at best impoverished or at worst narcissistic and even Gnostic if it does not at some point include reflection on children and procreation." Being human means that we are not in relationships of our own choosing, but of the choosing of God in Christ. The proper relationship between parents and children testifies to the relationship between God and humans because it is a relationship of God's choice, not ours.

There is an interesting commonality in the articles, though they were researched and written separately: sex and marriage are not about one's own desires and fulfillment, but are outwardly directed things, aimed toward the other person, toward growth, maturity, and deepened spirituality, for the benefit of the Church, with a view toward productive good, and for the sake of children. Sex and marriage are not about self-interest or self-fulfillment. This common thread stands against popular understandings and is immensely instructive for Christians and the Church.

I must acknowledge in particular the parish and people of St. Margaret's Anglican Church who supported the Consultation and worked to bring it about. This lively and growing congregation has wide interests, a leading one of which is its focus on "the life of the mind." Worshipers are called to participate in serious theological thinking—leading, of course, to action and care for people—when they assemble together as the Church. This deep thinking is led by the Rector, the Rev. Dr. David

Widdicombe, whose concerns for the gospel, the Church, preaching, and evangelism continue to arouse many to attention and action. The presenters at the St. Margaret's Consultation on Doctrine, Liturgy, and Preaching on the topic "Human Sexuality and the Nuptial Mystery" are to be thanked for their scholarly work, their lucid speaking and writing, and their generous interaction with many for whom the topics are difficult. Similarly, the audiences and interlocutors are to be thanked for their attention and dialogue.

Roy R. Jeal

Précis

Preston Parsons

In the early years of the fifth century, St. Augustine and St. Jerome exchanged letters concerning a point of scriptural interpretation that had become so vexed that a mutual friend had even attacked Jerome with a sword. But the antagonism was unsustainable, and Jerome wrote to Augustine:

> . . . let us be done with such quarrelling; let there be sincere brotherliness between us; and henceforth let us exchange letters, not of controversy, but of mutual charity. . . . Let us, if you please, amuse ourselves in the field of Scripture without wounding each other.[1]

Augustine, responding to Jerome's hope for amusement on the field of Scripture, asked if Jerome would willingly share the fruits of his wisdom, erudition, application to study, enthusiasm, and genius, in order to help those who are engaged in "great and difficult investigations." If this is play, wrote Augustine, let's also not pretend that it is easy:

> If, however, perchance you selected the expression *"ludamus"* [let us amuse ourselves] because of the genial kindliness which befits discussion between loving friends, whether the matter

---

1. "Letters of St. Augustine," in *Nicene and Post-Nicene Fathers*, trans. J. G. Cunningham, First Series, vol. 1, ed. Philip Schaff (Buffalo: Christian Literature Publishing, 1887, reprint 2004) 349. Cunningham translates *ludamus* as "exercise ourselves." I have used "amuse ourselves," a legitimate rendering, for the sake of consistency with Augustine's reply. Special thanks to Donald McKenzie for helping me track down this reference.

debated be obvious and easy, or intricate and difficult, I beseech you to teach me how I may succeed in securing this. . . .[2]

I draw on this illustration to describe the spirit of the St. Margaret's Consultation on Doctrine, Liturgy, and Preaching, entitled "Human Sexuality and the Nuptial Mystery." It was in this spirit that we spent three days playing on the field of Scripture, investigating and interrogating our traditions of interpretation, recognizing that this playful investigation is difficult, all the time hoping to remain under the rule of friendship.

So, perhaps, in a time of our own vexation over the matter of sexuality and the Church, it should not be a surprise that friendship was one of the major themes of the consultation. Some of the questions raised were: How is marriage like friendship? Is marriage a particular kind of friendship? Does marriage assume something more than friendship, such as an openness to procreation? Are there other kinds of friendship that could be blessed by the Church? Is friendship comprehensive enough for the variety of relationships found within the Church?

There were many other topics covered by local Anglican theologians from the parishes of St. Margaret and St. Mary Magdalene, St. John's College, members of the Primate's Theological Commission, and plenary speakers Oliver O'Donovan, Ephraim Radner, and Bishop Victoria Matthews. But they are too many to name here. Suffice to say it was a fruitful consultation, and a helpful step back from the immediacy of win and lose resolutions on the floors of synods—as if there are ever only two avenues of enquiry into any particular point of doctrine. There is, rather, the possibility that we can play and amuse ourselves on the field of Scripture. Theological discourse, even in its difficulty, even when a topic is so thorny, ought to be enjoyed. It ought to be fun—difficult fun—a difficult fun that can be pursued under the rule of friendship.

This consultation made Augustine's vision of theological discourse a reality, at least for a moment. Let us hope for more opportunities such as this.

---

2. "Letters of St. Augustine," 350.

On the Nature of Desire

A Sermon on Ecclesiastes 12:1–8 and Proverbs 13:12

John Stafford

To preach on the weighty topic of the nature of desire at 8:30 in the morning means that a person has to reach into his inner Methodist where any time is a good time to direct the mind toward this elusive theme. One is tempted to get to the good stuff right off the top—sex I mean—get a bit carried away, say a few intemperate things, and pronounce the Bible crystal clear about those matters which, on other grounds, one might feel a little less than totally secure. But to start with sex as the basis for a theology of nuptial *mystery* is crude paganism—we will get to that eventually, but long after this sermon is over. What I'm looking for is a starting point and there are many to choose from. The starting point cannot be sex because it is but one of the many aspects of being human of which we shall be dispossessed in this life, and, like conflict, if we get to say how it begins, we do not always get to say how it will end. And it may be in saying, ". . . though our outer nature is wasting away, our inner nature is being renewed every day" (2 Cor 4:16), that St. Paul has actually drawn on the existential wisdom of Qoheleth, the author of Ecclesiastes, though *he* has seen what Qoheleth has not. So with respect to the implications of our "outer nature," Paul can appear simultaneously very vigorous and also, at times, remarkably relaxed about the implications.

Qoheleth has put his finger on the troubling matter of being human in which, long story short, we are walking, living, breathing organs of desire. And we are *not* necessarily more attuned to this when contemplating sex than when we may be contemplating the accumulation of wealth or some vague notion of happiness (never a laughing matter) that will satisfy us. Qoheleth directs us, overall, to the central problem of human desire, which is death, not sex; fear, not fulfilment. And he is not alone in identifying this—texts much more ancient than the biblical ones point to a similar deep-rooted anxiety that the best of circumstances and human choice only blurs. Even the assured wisdom of Proverbs gets a bit uneasy when discussion turns upon what happens when we do not get what we want or desire, perhaps because it is so hard to tell the two apart. So much so, that growth in spiritual maturity might just as easily be measured in terms of a person's considered acceptance of how the word "No," or at least, "Not yet," is heard.

The great con is that *sex* is *the* driving urge that conditions all we do. Rather, I think it is *fear*. Endless debates about accessible sex, I suggest, may not reflect the heart of human impulses at all. Open and candid discussion about sex, as it emerged in the last century especially following World War II, has not resolved core issues nor where we should situate sex in our larger experience. In other words, the alleged liberating claims of a new and mature appreciation of human sexuality and its nuptial delight (let alone mystery), may be nothing more than sleight of hand, be it the unexamined benefits of cohabitation ("Hey, why ruin a good thing by getting married?"), or a new sexual normality that relegates strong cautionary voices to a rolling of the eyes and the mindless use of conservative or (worse) fundamentalist labels.

But Hollywood gets it, pornographers get it, and pagans get it too. Both sex and death can be exploited in the same movie because they are associated. That being so, the thought-world of the book of Leviticus also considers this linkage normative. But, although they are associated, the one is not simply the obverse of the other. Nuptial pleasure does not automatically infer nuptial mystery. Sex is easily discerned; it is death that troubles both us and the writer of Ecclesiastes.

But to move this forward, the familiar Pauline analogue of Christ and the Church only works when there is a theology that situates desire *beyond* the reach of sex as our *primary* identity. We are confronted in our generation with an impasse in our theological anthropology of staggering proportions at least in part because biblical literacy is so poor, and we therefore find it hard to know what limits to draw around culturally informed biblical metaphors. Vague claims, for instance, that rehearse the Pauline allegory of man and woman in nuptial union as depicting Christ and the Church, can have us reeling in dismay at the possibility that the love of Christ for his own redeemed body is as potentially dysfunctional as some of the marriages that take place within it—who wants to go down that road too far in the absence of a coherent Christology? Surely Paul would *not* have considered his metaphor useful for marriage counselling—or would he? And what mutual hope we can benefit from in our time together is a sense of the theological priorities that head off the counsel of despair while drawing us towards a deeper discipleship through recognition of the overarching triumph of divine grace, the security of our election in Christ, and the joy inherent in God's achievement in the resurrection of Jesus. For since, as Churchill said to Parliament, "We are so near to defeat, can victory be far away?" Nonetheless, the topic of nuptial desire does need a starting point, and I choose not to *begin* with sex of any description, or even marriage, since while one is as easy as falling off a log, the other can be as difficult as shaping the log into a beautiful thing—yet it is marriage that provides the available metaphor, not sex.

The book of Ecclesiastes is about the confrontation of desire and death—that death confronts every imaginable good at one level or another. And by death, the writer does not limit himself to physical dissolution. Disappointment is a sort of death, and the extended contemplation of old age in chapter 12 merely serves to nail the argument that we are ultimately dispossessed of the most tangible evidences of our physical powers. And the worst of it is, there is no final way to fend off dissolution because the only true desire is life itself and that, from the perspective of our author, is denied us. To him, what is left is the fear of God, the keeping of the commandments, and the prospect of judgement since, echoing the Psalmist, "what can one give in exchange for his life?" (Ps 49:7). Well, that is one thing. But, for all this, we are made in God's image, eternity hard-wired into our thoughts (Eccl 3:11), with the capacity and aptness to vision a desired future, but not the ability bring it about. Our desires are, in effect, God-like, and we test them out all the time. But we are also troubled because we cannot obtain the greatest of all outcomes: to live forever. And when all strategic desires, alliances, and happy contemplations have been stripped away, as in Ecclesiastes 12, there remains the fear that lurks below them regardless—we will not live forever by the strength of our own magic nor the desires of our own making. Our aptness to desire the good may be unabated, but our noetic depravity will distort it and compromise our ability to love it and do it. At its worst, desire is the handmaid of fear; at its best, to paraphrase Hooker, the handmaid of truth ("Reason is the hand by which the Spirit leads us"—by which Hooker means "redeemed reason," not abstract Cartesian reason). Hence, urges Paul, "bring every thought captive to Christ" (2 Cor 10:4). For if we do not, we will remain blown about by "every wind of doctrine" (Eph 4:14), and life contains enough fears as it is. Both Donne and Hooker probe this. St. John of the Cross, the great divines also. The problem is, we die and as such, the attempt to constrain the pain of our dissolution through desires of our own making leads us further from the one narrative that can embrace us. So the paradox of desire is that it can flow both from a need to soothe fear, yet give voice to our most creative gifts, each requiring heavy emotional investment and discipline—no easy task. In some people, the tension is too great, rather like Tolstoy's Ivan Illyich who, in morbid disappointment, saw death as the spoiler of dreams and us at the mercy of the fates. What are we to do with desire? Why care since "a living dog is better than a dead lion" (Eccl 9:4) which the NRSV chapter heading unhelpfully reminds us is all about "taking life as it comes."

The writer of Ecclesiastes, having experimented with all life's options, must yield to the inevitable depictions of chapter 12, robbed of every vital physical good, where even the desire for a good night's sleep can't be met and where the one true thing lies so far outside us it feels like a cruelty. There is but one thing: sometimes we glimpse it—the one desire for union with God and participation in his life. It would be comfortable to know that some action of ours would lift us out of the dilemma of living in the midst of death, but it is not available to us. Qoheleth thought we should settle into a life of obedience and acceptance; so did Paul (1 Cor 7:10–39) and so did Jesus (Matt 7:12). This gives rise to the strange new concept that desire is best channelled through ideas of obedience and discipleship. And, ironically, if desire is a paradox, so is obedience—freedom through obedience is as strange to us as life through death.

But surely the point is that desires have necessary boundaries (nothing controversial about that) since we accept that in many other aspects of life. Even speaking about them is no easy matter in the absence of a serious theology of the body and an even more articulate Christology. So we want to move into a discussion about nuptial mystery and therefore must grapple a bit for appropriate language in the midst of complex and intricate behaviours and modes of thinking. And Paul himself is not endlessly prescriptive about how we should faithfully act out our discipleship—indeed he cannot be, because that would be fatal to his own claim of spiritual discernment. He merely assumes that all discernment will ultimately glorify Christ. He certainly cannot envision a desireless or passionless Christian, but he can envision a point at which desire pushes a person away from "good order and unhindered devotion to the Lord" (1 Cor 7:35). After all, Paul thought "the present form of this world is passing away" (1 Cor 7:31), and as a consequence, the only final reality was Christ (Col 2:17) and the only true goal was realised in new creation (Gal 6:15; 2 Cor 5:17) and our participation in it. Admittedly, Paul can say a few things that defy any easy response—can you really live in married union while not reckoning yourself to be married solely on the grounds of apocalyptic expectation—the "present crisis" as he describes it? But we can leave such matters to another time. Meantime, can we not acknowledge the gifts of faith that subordinate a too-ready acceptance of personal desire until properly tested in the crucible of theology?

To want and to need the nuptial comforts of embodiment lies fully within the normal powers given to us, though it is clear that they do not constitute a necessity. Nuptial desires are such that the God-like powers these seem to be, if mishandled, point not to our participation in God but our actual alienation. So there is a need for a theology of desire, and it is to be found in the larger narratives of Scripture. Qoheleth asked all the right questions because he understood the problem so clearly and, within his limited horizon, he gave the right responses, stopping just short of eating, drinking, and being merry as if there was no tomorrow. The gospel, however, provides the basis for just such a hope in the present and in the future, but it requires that we embrace a life of desire shaped after the manner of God's reconciling appeal to men and women. God, being the author of all good desires, seeks more for us than eye hath seen or the heart of man ever conceived.

DESIRE, VOCATION, and FRIENDSHIP
THE MYSTERIES OF HUMAN SEXUALITY

1

How Can We Frame the Right Questions?

Oliver O'Donovan

Martin Luther opens his Sermon on *The Estate of Marriage* with the observation that each of us has a sex. We find ourselves with our sex and can do nothing to change it, and we all have relations with the same and the other sex, from which we cannot by any means extricate ourselves. "Therefore, each one of us must have the kind of body God has created for us. I cannot make myself a woman, nor can you make yourself a man; we do not have that power. But we are exactly as he created us: I a man and you a woman. Moreover, he wills to have his excellent handiwork honored as his divine creation, and not despised."[1] Naïve this may seem, but for a place to begin there are few better. It draws our attention to the question that comes first, before marriage and the blessing of procreation pronounced on man and woman, before "sexuality" and the range of emotional responses and habitual reflexes that may be governed by our sex. Before we can talk of the meeting of the sexes, before we can talk of the experience of being sexed, we must recognise the *being* of the sexes.

This starting point has the additional benefit of forcing us out of the observer's and into the existential point of view. To discuss sex well, we must discuss it not as sociologists, amateur or professional, not as behavioural psychologists, conservative or radical, but with a sense that

---

1. *Luther's Works*, trans. Walther I. Brandt, vol. 45 (St. Louis: Concordia, 1966) 17.

our own being is engaged. Pornography panders to the temptation to treat sexual experience as a transitory entertainment we may look in on from time to time and then go on with our lives unaffected. And it can gain support from ways of discussing sex that fail of existential seriousness. These include not only the detachment of the would-be human-scientist, but the managerial control of the pastoral professional, who, in eagerness to relieve the burden of guilt with minimum fuss, may all too quickly encourage the idea that anything that has to do with sex is superficial and unimportant. From the point of view of the last judgment, of course, it may well be so. But so are many other things we are bound to take seriously in the course of living our lives. Our instincts tell us that the problem of sexual self-possession is close to the heart of the question of virtue; that is to say, it deeply concerns how we are to live our lives as meaningful and worthwhile wholes.

This instinctual association of sex with virtue has been articulated within the ordered tradition of Christian teaching, where it has been situated within the frame of divine grace and the redemption of broken humanity. That is why it is *in the Church* that the anguished debate goes on in our own times about the meaning and value of gay sex. Apparently there is no other ordered discourse for which the question of virtue and the question of sexual self-possession are woven together as they are in the Church's discourse, and as they certainly are in our experience of ourselves. This much at least, then, must be said in the Church's favor, before we get into the usual hand-wringing and deploring: whether persuasively or unpersuasively, perceptively or unperceptively, the Church treats seriously of difficulties that arise in all seriousness within lived human experience. There is nothing to be ashamed of in the bare fact of the Church's engagement, often unsupported, with this debate.

I want to begin by saying a word about one of many books that has appeared in recent years advocating a permissive approach to same-sex relations. It is a book I take to be of intellectual seriousness, a worthy statement of the kind of approach it favours. It is *The Ethics of Sex* by Mark D. Jordan.[2] In this context I cannot do justice to its strengths as the product of a lively and creative intelligence, but only give a rough idea of how its angle of vision on the question lies. In picking it out for discussion I do not mean to suggest that its angle of vision is that of all gay Christians, or even most. I choose it for three reasons. The first is simply that there

---

2. Mark D. Jordan, *The Ethics of Sex* (Oxford: Blackwell, 2002).

ought always to be *some* clearly stated position on the table when non-gay Christians discuss this topic, since otherwise they fall into the way of depicting the gay Christian to fit their own fears or theories. This debate would make more progress, I think, if everybody who joined in would follow this simple precaution. No contribution can bring us further forward if it represents its opponents unbelievably. The second reason is that it is specially important to attend to what *gay* Christians say about their position, not merely to what *pro-gay* Christians say. The advocacy of the cause has often fallen to non-gay Christians of liberal convictions, who bring to the discussion their own agenda, usually of an emancipationist or rights-oriented kind, and are more interested in gays as victims of persecution than as bearers of a distinct experience that can be of importance and interest in its own right. The voice of Mark Jordan brings a very different set of concerns to the fore from such liberal advocates as my former colleague Marilyn McCord Adams.[3] Non-gays need to attend to what is offered for Christian understanding out of the gay experience. My third reason is that this book sets a high value on thematizing the experience of sexuality within a context of prayer and discipleship. Though passionately critical of much traditional teaching, it makes no suggestion that there ought to be no Christian teaching on this subject, nor does it ever suggest that the controversy is about nothing at all. It hopes to free what Christians think and say and teach about sex from certain supposed shackles and inhibitions; it does not hope to free Christians from thinking and speaking and teaching about sex altogether.

Jordan describes his contribution as an "attack upon Christendom." Yet he does not wish his attack to be taken for an *angry* one. Much that parades as "gay" comes out, in fact, as sullen and sour. But this, he hopes, is to be a *happy* attack, designed to free Christian sexual ethics from the unenviable fate that has befallen it of being a "handbook for the police." Studying the history of the Christian tradition, Jordan discovers there a wide variety of "sexual speeches," as he calls them, which have in common a concern to uphold a certain regulation of sexuality. The account he gives of this is heavily dependent on Michel Foucault, whose three "hypotheses" about the history of the Western sexual tradition Jordan takes up with approval: 1) the West has over-produced discourse about

---

3. See, for example, Marilyn McCord Adams, "Faithfulness in Crisis" in *Gays and the Future of Anglicanism*, eds. Andrew Linzey and Richard Kirke (Winchester: O Books, 2005) 70–80.

sex; 2) the discourse has very quickly taken a scientific form—in contrast to the Eastern "art of the erotic"; 3) the demands of a science of sex have been imposed by an ensemble of mechanisms of power, the pastorate. But, Jordan proceeds, the situation has radically altered now that the churches have fallen from their positions of power. The churches' relation to secular bureaucracies in the exercise of "biopower" has been turned upside down. "National and transnational bureaucracies are ever more efficiently involved in the regulation of citizen-sexuality," he tells us; and the task of the churches in this situation is not to maintain an ever-shrinking slice of the regulatory cake, but to warn people against docility.[4] There is no place, he insists, for talk of "rights." Codifying rights is simply the obverse of codifying sins. What is at fault is precisely the exercise of *codification*. Christian sexual ethics has to be the salvific and liberating teaching of God displayed through the sexual lives of Christians.

Jordan believes that we now stand at the beginning of a new, revolutionary Christian sexual ethics. But how can the revolution take responsibility for the Christian past? Christian discourse on sex has revolved around two themes, nature and shame. But "nature" is an ideology, immune from refutation. The rule must be: respond not to what it says, but to how it operates. So the past discourses must be dumped and a new theological strategy put in place, which is to attend to the demands of *negative* or *apophatic* theology. God teaches mankind progressively and in parables. More time is needed, then, to see what God is teaching in the sexual lives of Christian believers, but in the meantime Christian ethics has something to do as well as attacking Christendom. It must be fashioning hopeful speeches to replace the "ugly" ones of the past, speeches whose theme is *pleasure*.[5] Christian writers of the past have pronounced "calumnies" about erotic pleasure. But pleasure should be understood as an approach to the original created order. There are spiritual resources within the Christian tradition for celebrating pleasure: mystical writings are famously erotic, a fact that should not be explained away as mere allegory. Liturgical worship is full of physical pleasures of sound and sight. Our union with God in prayer is the fulfilment of our capacity for erotic pleasure. Intense private prayer resembles masturbation, while sado-masochistic satisfaction resembles ascetic discipline. Even moral theology, Jordan promises—and how can I be indifferent to

---

4. Jordan, *Ethics of Sex*, 133f.
5. Ibid., 155ff.

this?—may be beautiful in its rhetorical craft and persuasive force. But pleasure is not the end of it. Talk about sex has always been about *identities*, and the task of the new Christian ethic is to construct Christian identities within which the erotic is fully integrated.

Let me offer three preliminary words of general comment about this program, before I pursue some of the major questions it raises in a less direct way. First of all (and to repeat), it is not a manifesto about justice or rights or remedying the historical wrongs of a persecuted class. The agenda Jordan sets before us is that of thinking about our common sexuality, and how we may relate communally to it. His liberating word is intended to be no less liberating for non-gays than for gays. He hopes to persuade us simply that within the common life of the Spirit regulation is inappropriate and unnecessary, as well for the one class as for the other.

In the second place, I think there can still be little surprise if, despite the emollient tone of this, an approach presented in these terms ends up at the center of an almighty row. Jordan himself is quite unsurprised. "How can issues of sexual ethics prove so divisive?" he asks; and replies, "The question ought rather to be: When have they not?"[6] Christian sexual ethics are divisive because they are bound up in questions of the Church, questions of nature and history, and questions about God. The questions, for Jordan, are nothing if not deeply theological, and the answers offered deeply revisionist and antinomian.

Thirdly, there is assumed in his approach a distinctive view of the Church. Without prejudice one might say that Jordan offers a Quaker answer to an ultramontane problem: he conceives the Church as a godly conversation of the like-minded, with no noticeable place for institutional answerability. The longing for discipline is, he thinks, something near to the original sin, a fatal flaw that has turned the Church from its first purity. And here he quickly makes common cause with the post-Catholic sociology of Foucault, for whom the traditional civilization of the West—a vaguely defined area that sometimes seems to end at Belgrade, sometimes at Bombay—is essentially Catholic Christianity writ large. It is quite difficult for well-informed Anglicans (who, for the most part, formed the original audience of this essay) to see their own culture in this supposedly common Western past. Much is, and much has been, amiss in the Anglican world, and it has not been without its

6. Ibid., 173.

own arbitrary exercises of power. But that moral theology ever served as a handbook for the police is not a proposition Anglican historians are likely to entertain for very long. The question arises, then, whether the liberation on offer actually delivers us from any historical experience.

After these purely introductory observations about Mark Jordan's book, I want to turn aside, not to leave his substantive proposals behind, but to widen the range of participation in the discussion. That he speaks out of a recognizable strand of gay thinking is guaranteed, I think, by his heavy dependence upon Foucault, who has become for gays something of what Augustine used to be for Western Christians—the thinker whose authority must be claimed, even in contradiction to his actual views! But I do not think his voice is representative of all, or most, gay Christian voices; or, at any rate, I do not think that a non-gay commentator has a right to assume this. Gay Christians must speak for themselves, and not be spoken for by me or anyone else. If we are to think ahead to that great discussion that the churches still need to learn how to have, we must open the door, at least, to the possibility of positions taken by gay Christians that are less deeply revisionist. To do otherwise would be to force them into a radical corner, which would not be helpful for them and would be unhelpful in the long run for orthodox Christianity. Christian orthodoxy, using the term in its Western sense, with a lower-case "o," is a uniting, centripetal force. The first thing it behoves those who care about orthodoxy to do is to invite all who can, and will, to associate themselves with their confession of faith.

It was for that reason that a decade or so ago a group of theologians in Britain with whom I was associated, in drafting a document on this subject that was called *The St. Andrew's Day Statement*, framed it in the form of a creed with a commentary, hoping that in that way they might encourage gay voices to identify, to the extent that they could, with their own concern for the integrity of Christian doctrine and practice, and that they might establish whether the gap between orthodox and gay might be measured in inches rather than miles.[7] The time was not ripe, as it turned out, for that invitation to be heard or understood. But it is still supremely important for it to be issued. So in what follows I want to frame five questions, which should be taken as addressed to gay

---

7. This text is found in Timothy Bradshaw, ed., *The Way Forward?: Christian Voices on Homosexuality and the Church* (London: Hodder & Stoughton, 2003) 5–11. Online: http://www.anglicancommunion.org/listening/book_resources/docs/St%20Andrew's%20Day%20Statement.pdf.

Christians in the hearing of the Church in general, seeking to *clarify* their relation to Christian understandings historically and ecumenically accepted by the catholic Church. The revisionist posture of Mark Jordan can thus be treated as a boundary line, a possible horizon, on which, or short of which, gays may locate themselves, as they judge fit, in relation to the Church's faith as traditionally taught and practiced.

One further prefatory word about the point of all this and how we go about it: the point of this discussion is not to insinuate in the subtlest possible way what I myself think about gay sexual relations. A number of those who commented on *The St. Andrew's Day Statement,* unable to believe that an open invitation from one set of convictions to another could be openly meant, triumphantly uncovered messages between the lines which, had they looked, they could have found written quite plainly *on* the lines. Just to save you the burden of reading between *my* lines, I shall state directly the view I take of the sexuality issue, and get it out of the way. I am a traditional Christian, who believes that God created man and woman for one another and that marriage and singleness are the two forms of life within which a vocation may be discerned. So what is there left to discuss? A very great deal. There is much that our age does not understand about itself and the peculiar shape that some of its moral choices take in distinction from those faced by ages that have gone before. Serious and attentive listening to a range of experiences is a necessary precondition for any kind of discernment and discrimination. Dialogue is the only way that either side can, as it were, come *to understand the truth of its own position.* It was disappointing that our attempt to speak to gay Christians back in 1997 did not elicit the kind of dialogical response that we were looking for. Evidently we had not found a way of speaking that could make our intentions clearly understood. It was disappointing to encounter what sometimes appeared as an unreadiness to hear, so that what might have emerged from clear speaking and clear listening was lost, which was an opportunity for the church to *learn* more about the question it faces. What is good *listening*? That term is much misunderstood. It is not a matter of agreeing, which would be to capitulate before the discussion starts. It is not a matter of sympathy, as one might feel for suffering. It is not a matter of simply enduring while the opponent talks. It is a matter of *getting one's mind round* a position that one does not hold. The good listener can give as clear an account of the opponent's views, and the reasons for holding it, as the opponent can give. And that is seriously difficult, requiring us, as the phrase goes, to "leave our comfort zone," a zone constructed out of a reassuringly diminishing view of the opposition we have to face.

I

The first question concerns creation: is "homosexual" a natural form? Aristophanes' speech in Plato's *Symposium* represents the two kinds of homosexual mythically as present in nature just like the two kinds of heterosexual, but this was in the context of thinking that the individual, with his or her sexual longing, was the result of a fall from an originally tri-morphic bi-personal unity. What can we make of this within the context of a belief in divine creation? When the creation narrative tells us, "male and female created he them," are we to expand that to mean: "male, both homosexual and heterosexual according to their kinds, and female, both homosexual and heterosexual according to their kinds, created he them"? And what, in addition, are we to make of male and female bisexuals, a form unacknowledged by Plato's Aristophanes?

The alternative to understanding homosexuality as a natural form is to understand it as something like a *happening*, an *event* in the sexual history of the race, which has "developed" or "emerged," like literacy or technology. So a different, but closely related question would be this: does the noun "homosexual" function like the noun "man," or like the noun "traveller"? You can encounter a man; you can encounter a traveller. But "man" names a *way of being*, "travelling" names a *way of doing*. "Traveller" is a term for a man or a woman who happens, at the moment in question, to be engaged in travelling. The *St. Andrews Day Statement* encountered some criticism for saying that there was no such thing as "a" homosexual or "a" heterosexual. The inverted commas placed around the indefinite articles were a way of making the point that the *ontological status* of these designations of human sexuality was not that of a substance. They were *qualifications* of men and women.

Among the most straightforward advocates of what we may call the four-sex view can be numbered, unexpectedly, the Church of England bishops of twenty years ago, who, in a document called *Issues in Human Sexuality*, conservative in tendency and something of an iconic hate-object for gay and liberal Christians, addressed some strikingly unconservative advice to bisexuals: "The Church's guidance to bisexual Christians," they wrote, "is that if they are capable of heterophile relationships and of satisfaction within them, they should follow the way of holiness in either celibacy or abstinence or heterosexual marriage. In the situation of the bisexual it can also be that counselling will help the person concerned to discover the truth of their personality and to achieve a degree of inner healing."[8] Apparently, homosexuality could be the truth of someone's personality, but bisexuality could not be. Bisexuality needed healing, homosexuality did not. That is to follow the logic of calling homosexuality a natural form very strictly: God created four sexes—*and no more than four!*

There is no ambiguity about the answer given to this question by the tradition following Foucault. An ontological concept of homosexuality was associated with what it called the "medicalization" of sex, typified by the nineteenth-century idea of the "true homosexual" as opposed to various kinds of pseudo-homosexual. For Foucault and his followers this was essentially an ideological mystification. A gay identity arose as a historical possibility at a certain juncture—a dictum popularly attributed to Foucault asserts that sex began in the sixteenth century, sexuality in the nineteenth—and had to be embraced and constructed as an act of self-creation. The questions—all the questions—are ultimately phenomenological and historical. Foucault was dismissive of those who claimed respect for their homosexuality on the ground that it was natural. But an uncompromising historicism is not easy to carry through, whether philosophically or, especially, theologically. Not even Mark Jordan is prepared to deny himself the odd mention of creation-order. Yet there is something important to be learned from it. Orthodox Christian discussion of God's finished work of creation was never in direct competition with talk of God's ongoing providence. A discussion of the order of created reality will necessarily lead on to a discussion of how created structures take form in time as history. Without that, it can hardly be the *same* creation we are talking about when we speak of original creation, fallen creation, redeemed creation, and perfected creation. Salvation history is the very structure of the Christian message, and that must be at once the history of a *saved creation* and the *history of the saving* of creation. So it is not uncommon to find theologians differentiating what belongs essentially to the creation from what belongs to history. We should not be surprised, then, at the need to discern a *history* of sex that elaborates

---

8. *Issues in Human Sexuality: A Statement by the House of Bishop* (London: Church House, 1991) 42.

a *nature* of sex—a history that includes, of course, all kinds of perversion and exploitation, but which may also include (can we rule this out *a priori*?) differentiations, elaborations, complexifications that are essentially constructive. Even the married–single alternative presented by the New Testament is a salvation-historical development upon the "male and female" of Genesis.

We do not, then, have to embrace the all-out historicism of Foucault if we are to find value in the suggestion that sex is *also* historically conditioned, and to a certain extent *plastic* to the virtues and moral self-disposal of agents. That is one of the things that may be meant, perhaps, by that "nineteenth-century" idea, sexuality. What presents itself to us as homosexuality today may be, and in some respects surely is, distinctively *of our time*. It has many unprecedented features. If we were to agree on that point, some quite serious changes might follow for the way either side in the current debate was presented. It would put a stop to the history-of-persecution style of gay advocacy. The gay historicist is not in a position to indulge the pathos of gays persecuted throughout the ages; in this respect gay advocacy could profitably learn from second-generation feminism. And in proposing a situation that is in important respects new, some acknowledgment could also surely be given to the need for patience in coming to a clear assessment of it. The non-gay, on the other hand, will have to admit that new questions present themselves, that the question of contemporary homosexuality is not simply self-answering, just as the question of genetic engineering is not simply self-answering, and the formulations of the Scriptures and the Church's past, though a necessary and essential starting point, with which we must keep faith in thinking about our contemporary situation, will not necessarily yield a conclusive answer.

II

The second question concerns the Incarnation. For there is a special problem for Christian faith in all-out historicism: if the narrative of saving history is destroyed from one side by the refusal to accommodate history, it is destroyed from the other side by a refusal to accommodate created nature. There is no saving history if there is no nature to be saved. But the doctrines of creation and history join essentially at the saving disclosure of God within the human nature of Jesus of Nazareth. What, then, will a gay thinker make of this conjuncture of nature and history? We often hear it suggested that faith in the Incarnation has the simple implication that we must take the world together with its fleshly, physical character seriously. We sometimes hear it suggested, too, in a polemical vein, that those who oppose the gay cause do so simply from disgust at the flesh, springing from a world-rejecting and defective doctrine of the Incarnation. The first thing to say about this is that neither in the discussion of sexual conduct nor in the discussion of the Incarnation is *flesh* the chief focus of attention—to that point we shall return. The second is that the Incarnation is not merely an affirmation of human existence in its worldly aspects. As Augustine said in response to Pelagius, divine grace is not simply a matter of how human nature is constituted, but of how it is healed.[9] The Incarnation also, and supremely, *shapes the history of the world*, which turns around the saving and transforming events of the first century. Together with those events, and inseparable from them, are their context and the literary testimony to them and their context: the ancient race of Israel, on the one hand, together with its Scriptures, and the apostolic writings on the other.

The anxiety has been raised in orthodox circles that revisionism over homosexuality fronts for a much wider theological revisionism: for marginalization of the historical Incarnation and the revival of Unitarianism. For myself I do not feel able to form a judgment about how realistic this anxiety really is. Mark Jordan is an example, not uncommon perhaps, of a theologian who, while not actually affording direct grounds for it, does little to allay it. His proposal for an apophatic theology could seem to be a way of sidelining not only the tradition but also the scriptural roots of the tradition. If not Christ himself, at least a great deal about him—his teachings (including the exacting word on divorce and remarriage) and the testimony of his contemporary Christian interpreters—seem to fall foul of a revolutionary sense that everything important is beginning anew. So the second question that needs to be engaged between gay and non-gay thinkers is how to clarify the place that the historical Incarnation of God in Christ holds in Christian thinking.

III

The third question concerns the notion of identity. "Nature" specifies features we have in common with others, generically; "identity" particularizes those features within the existence of a unique individual

---

9. Augustine *On Nature and Grace* 11.12.

subject. My "identity" is my grasp of myself, the essence of what I have at my disposal in the living of my life. If "nature" represents the given conditions of my existence, which I may or may not recognize but can do nothing about, "identity" speaks of what I make of myself within those conditions. The *St. Andrew's Day Statement* was critical of the idea of homosexuality as an identity, and one of the useful points that came out of subsequent exchanges, a point made by the present Archbishop of Canterbury, was that there is more than one way of deploying the term "identity."[10] The drafters of the Statement had in their sights a somewhat Freudian conception, in which sexuality played a *foundational role* in the person one was to be. The language of "coming out" and "discovering the truth of my personality" seemed to be premised on the myth of a secret inmost shrine located in the powers of sex, which amounted, in their view, to an idolatry of sexuality. It is of interest, then, that Jordan uses the term in a different way. Religious talk about sex, he says, aims to *shape* identities and it ought to be talk that is likely to shape identities that properly accommodate and integrate the erotic. Without getting into the much more vexing question of what those identities may look like in detail, this formulation, at least, does not make totalitarian claims for sexuality.

If we gloss his use of the phrase "constructing identity" with the traditional phrase "forming character," his recommendation may even sound pretty old-fashioned: sex has to do with virtue, i.e., with living life with integrity, and life cannot be lived with integrity if the erotic (by which I hope he means powers not only of body but of mind) have not been assigned their proper place. It may be that this, too, is not the only way to understand gay talk about identity. I have suggested in the past that it might correspond to the less exclusively moral concept of *vocation*: my vocation is the human life that I, in all the particularity of my unique subjectivity and my unique historical setting, am summoned by God to realize—not merely in respect of the moral characteristics that are open to me to develop, but in respect of the particular courses of action that I undertake and no one else does.

The question to be raised with gay theologians, then, is how they can conceive their vision of an integrated Christian identity *both* in relation to the central theological concepts of conversion, identity, and sanctification *and* in relation to a vocation to serve others. Here is a suggestion

10. Rowan Williams, "Knowing Myself in Christ," in *The Way Forward?* ed. Bradshaw, 12–19.

from the gay philosopher, Mark Vernon: "There is a job for gay men to do," he writes. "The job for gay men is to open up closed possibilities of relationship to expansive possibilities of friendship."[11] I quote that, not to commend it as such, or even to agree with it, but to illustrate the *kind* of proposition that could make sense of the contemporary homosexual disposition as a vocation within the contemporary world. Answers like that, though perhaps different from it, need to be sought and explored.

IV

The fourth question concerns the erotic. If I were asked to say for myself what positive contribution the whole gay experiment could make to ecumenical theology, I might hazard a hope that it could be in this area. Gay theologians have begun to take up the topic of the erotic in a positive tone, in sharp contrast to the negativity that prevailed in the mid-twentieth century, for example, in Nygren's famous work, *Agape and Eros*. The seriousness of a gay theologian must be judged by the intention to address the whole Church about its good news. Mark Jordan's account of eros represents the evangelical side of his task, as he conceives it. As I have already commented, it is antinomian. Evangelical enthusiasms sometimes are, but that may turn out to be a corrigible fault.

On the evidence of what Jordan has to tell us, however, the contribution to a theology of eros has a very long way to go if it is even to recover ground that was perfectly familiar to Plato and to the Christian theologians in the Greek tradition indirectly influenced by him. Jordan is aware of material to be quarried in the mystical tradition, but his failure to make much of it is evidenced in a very impoverished erotic vocabulary. At the center of his account, hardly distinguished from eros, is "pleasure," which does a great deal, too much indeed, of the work. When the reference of this term slides without comment from the physical release of an orgasm to the visual delightfulness of liturgical vestments or the aural delight of polyphonic singing, let alone to the intellectual satisfaction of contemplating truth, the incongruities simply beg the question. Making analogical connexions between unlikely things can be illuminating. But the connections must actually be *made,* and in order to make them, the gay theologian needs to deploy with some self-conscious discipline the whole range of concepts that deal with human aspiration and satisfaction: happiness, contentment, fulfilment, self-realization,

---

11. Mark Vernon, *The Philosophy of Friendship* (New York: Palgrave, 2005) 134.

etc. The ancient world knew that pleasure alone could not carry the burden of an account of what human beings strive for, or even what they self-consciously desire.

At the risk of impudently telling gay theologians what to think, let me just point in one direction. To talk about eros requires us to talk about the *imagination,* and especially the visual imagination. Eros is directed to beauty; it is the point at which aesthetic perception plays a constitutive role in forming our loves. Beauty is the power that draws us out of ourselves towards the transcendent, but it is always encountered in some concrete object, characteristically a person. The erotic imagination is an analogical imagination, making a two-way connection between universal beauty and the particular loved object. The particular human body is seen in terms of other non-human beauties, material, intellectual, spiritual, while other beauties are seen in terms of a particular human body. "Your rounded thighs are like jewels. . . . Your navel is a rounded bowl that never lacks mixed wine," we read in the Song of Songs (7:1f), and though the aesthetic imagery is exotic to our taste, the rhetorical strategy is familiar enough: the attractiveness of the human body is constructed of beauties derived from the world around it. The contrary movement is illustrated by the love-story of Nabal and Abigail in 1 Samuel 25, which is an allegory of how David was transformed from a guerrilla chief into a true king. Abigail, the gracious wife of Nabal, "the fool," successfully diverts David's fury at Nabal's obstruction, and so prevents him from carrying out a revenge-massacre; whereupon, the fool conveniently dying of his humiliation, David marries the lovely widow. It is an erotic story about a charming and virtuous woman who wins the love of a strong man; but since Abigail represents in her person the virtues of discretion and diplomacy needed by a king, it is also a story of how a warrior was formed for political responsibility by the softening and civilizing features of a virtuous and peaceable society.

Is it the *erotic-aesthetic,* then, rather than the *sexual,* that lies at the heart of the gay agenda? Is the question not, after all, about a section of the human race that is different from the rest of us and must be allowed fulfillment on its own terms, but, asked more hopefully, about a new challenge to a culture become too sheerly materialistic and sensual, having lost its contact with the realm of sensibility and feeling? Do gays, in effect, want to take up John Milbank's claim that a morality must be in some sense an aesthetic morality, a construal of the shape of things which discovers beauty? Is the purpose to offer us all an *éducation sentimentale*? If so, then we must look for a more serious engagement than we find in Jordan with the *intellectual* problems that befall eros. We cannot be content to be told of a simple revaluation of the flesh: an Apollinarian Incarnation to resolve the problems of a Gnostic orthodoxy. It was not the flesh that worried Saint Paul; it was what he called "the mind of the flesh," i.e., the *intellectual* construction of the world on reductionist sensualist and materialist lines, standing in the way of an adequate aesthetics.

V

It is as we think this question through to its logical end that the fifth question follows: *What disciplines of responsible expression may be given to the love between same-sex partners?* If the truth of the gay orientation lies in the realm of erotic responsiveness, and has to do with imagination and feeling, then the disciplines of self-disposal become the chief object of enquiry. That, at any rate, was how it appeared to the mystical writers, who were the most important *moral* students of the erotic. The capacity to see truly is related to virtue; it is acquired by serious attention to the way life is lived. There can be nothing glib or easy in the transition from emotional responsiveness to erotic responsibility. Our active life has to be shaped by the understanding, attentive to the realities, social and personal, of those with whom we communicate. The patterns of living that fit us to pursue and communicate a love of beauty have to be formed and learned. None of us sets out fully armed with a knowledge of how to show and accept love appropriately. Our instincts and inclinations are important, but they frame the question, they do not answer it. It must surely be unthinkable for a seriously erotic Christianity to resort to the dismissive gestures of antinomianism. It has to be able to appropriate the laws of love if it is to cut out a path of moral deliberation leading from love-of-beauty to action. The aesthetic that takes a short cut at this point simply forces the concreteness of the beloved into some abstract ideal of beauty that erotic fancy has come up with. And that is emotional exploitation.

I do not think we can simply tell gay thinkers that the answer lies with the traditional moral rules that Christians have always understood to govern sexual encounter. They find these problematic; that was the starting-point of the discussion. What we can do is to invite them to reappraise these rules in the light of their own need to trace the outlines of an ethic of sexual encounter. Their plausibility will, in the end, turn on whether they have anything to offer a young person seeking for his or her way in life, other than an invitation to be subversive. The "creative subversion" of gay friendship, of which Mark Vernon speaks, is an oxymoron needing to be resolved. Subversiveness is not in itself creative. If a genuinely creative innovation proves subversive, that means there was something in need of subversion, but it is the creativity that does the subverting, not the subversiveness the creating. Furthermore any given form of subversiveness runs out of steam, perhaps quite quickly. Society's most basic defense mechanism is to neutralize subversive impulses by making them respectable. The only surprising thing about how this has occurred in the case of homosexuality is its sheer speed, with the ironic result that those gays who depend in any measure on social hostility to define their identity are having to go much further in search of it. If, on the other hand, gays can find a way of addressing the young about what it means to pursue goals that go beyond the sensual or the emotional while not denying those spheres of experience, then they will have been helpful in ways from which non-gays, too, may learn. If they cannot, it will not matter very much what is said in reply to them, for they will lack the power to inspire, their particular subversive fashion will pass, and their place will see them no more.

The important thing to ask gay thinkers, then, is what shape such an erotic discipline of life might take, a discipline that they would wish to urge on homosexual Christians, not as lawmakers, not even as pastors, but simply as caring friends. One such proposal, of course, is on the table. It has the merit of being very clear and precise. It is that the structure of such relations should be that of exclusive marriage, lifelong and indissoluble, a simple extension of the sacrament of marriage as it has hitherto been recognized, between two persons of the same sex. It would include the bars of affinity and consanguinity, the ideal of restricting sexual intimacy to the context of marriage, and so on. In England a proposal of this kind is associated especially with the name of Jeffrey John, Dean of St. Albans. One of the things that makes the gay phenomenon of our age wholly distinct from its antecedents is an interest in the idea of homosexual marriage and family, including childrearing. But some who speak out of the gay culture seriously distrust the idea of taking marriage as a model. The analogy between homosexual and heterosexual unions, they think, can only be a formal and abstract one, ignoring what is really distinctive about the male-to-male relations and female-to-female. To these it seems that the model of *friendship* is much more suited to meet the need to give shape to same-sex relations, a point of view represented, in the context of a wide-ranging treatment of friendship, by Mark Vernon. If, as I am inclined to suspect, this is more sensitive to the elements both of competitiveness and task-oriented cooperativeness that same-sex friendships are likely to embody, especially among men, it remains more under-specified ethically, more purely in the realm of experiment.

It is not up to me, or to any non-gay, to instruct gays on the best way to think of their relationships. What the wider Church can do is to be a friendly sounding board for the explorations that gays need to make, and with that provide a reality check for speculative self-depictions that, by the very nature of the question, are always likely to be in danger of becoming fantastic. Can we envisage a friendly partnership in which the Church becomes, as it were, the confidant to the questions gay Christians ask about themselves? Only, I think, on two conditions. One is that the *question* of the gay experience—a matter on which I think, even now, there is little objective knowledge to be had—must be of interest and concern to the Church as a question about our common humanity. It is no good the Church taking the gays up as a cause to fight for—just another oppressed tribe in need of emancipation. The other is that gays must be content for the Church to take them as they are, in the midst of exploration and experiment, not as they would like to be, in a state of achieved self-understanding. That gays should be pastorally accommodated within the Church in some sensitive way is necessary to any dialogue, but while the questions remain open, that accommodation is bound to be *ad hoc*. The Church can hardly be asked to sign up in advance to general changes in teaching and practice that would only make sense on the assumption that we had well-understood answers, when in fact we have only rather less-well-understood questions.

The biggest obstacle to open and fruitful conversation is an atmosphere of incrimination, whether the incrimination of gays as wilfully deviant, the incrimination of the Church as constitutionally homophobic, or the incrimination of past generations of Christians by the present-day Christians as guilty of sins they hardly had the imagination or opportunity to commit. Whoever we are that incriminate and whoever the targets of our incrimination, incrimination means disclaiming responsibility for the challenge faced by our age, laying it on others' shoulders to ask and seek answers to the questions that humanity requires should not be ignored.

2

Ideology, Argumentation, and Social Direction in Romans 1

Roy R. Jeal

My task is to examine and interpret the foundational biblical material that informs our topics: "human sexuality" and the "nuptial mystery."[1] The obvious first step is to determine where to look in the Bible in order to have productive discussion. Many passages are employed to make one point or another opposing point in the current dialogues, debates, and arguments, and deciding where to begin is itself a significant undertaking.[2] Romans 1, however, is the central New Testament text that must be considered in order to come to an understanding of a biblical theory, doctrine, or worldview that is relevant to Christian and Church discussions about homoerotic behaviors and same-sex relation-

---

1. Interpretation is to be assumed whenever we look at texts or use words at all. Interpretation is basic to human existence. We all do it in multiple ways all the time.

2. Here we may be reminded of the Sufi story about a man searching frantically in the street for a lost key. Various neighbors began to assist in the search, but no one could find the missing key. Eventually a friend asked, "Where did you lose the key?" and the man replied, "I lost it in my house." "Then why are you searching for it in the street?" The man replied, "Because that is where the light is." Many things are to be found not in the light but in dark and obscure and sometimes surprising corners of texts and thoughts and understandings. It is important to start in the right places. This requires discernment, time and energy. What are the right places? Christians start in scripture.

ships.[3] It is not my task to enter the political and biological debates, even though touching on them is inevitable at some points. It is not my task to enter the more highly charged and emotional debates about people whom we know and love. My task is to examine the Scripture, in this case Romans 1—something the Church must always do. The Bible *is* the authoritative *text*,[4] "God's word written,"[5] containing "all things necessary to salvation."[6] The Bible is *the primary source material* for what we know about the promises to and the expectations of ancient Israel regarding the coming of the kingdom of God and the Messiah, of our knowledge of Jesus of Nazareth, the Messiah, of redemption, of the earliest church, and of apostolic teaching. One thing that cannot change for Christians is acceptance of the Bible as Scripture and as authoritative. What has certainly changed, and will continue to change, is people's understanding of the Bible, of what it means and how it is to be understood and actually used as the authoritative word.[7] Interpretations of the Bible and of its various parts move and change through a range of eras, socio-cultural pressures, interpretive methodologies, and theological, philosophical, and political viewpoints. Nevertheless, the Bible may not be treated as a mere *object* or as an *artifact* from the past that, while interesting and having historic, historical, and literary value, has little direct relevance to faith or theology or ethics or the realities of a pluralistic, yet strangely individualistic, time.[8] Modern and postmodern notions of human needs and human rights do not trump Christ, Christian faith, Christian theology, or Christian Scripture. So, along with the foundational interpretive concerns about what Paul said and what is meant in Romans 1, lies the question of whether (Anglican) Christians

---

3. We do not properly begin with, say, Lev 18:22; 20:13 or 1 Cor 6:9, passages that, particularly when read out of context and without appropriate regard for the presuppositions of the readers themselves, often arouse huge amounts of emotion and discussions that generate more heat than light.

4. Authority resides, of course, in Christ as head of the Church. The Bible may not be set in the place of Christ.

5. Article 20 of the Articles of Religion.

6. Article 6 of the Articles of Religion.

7. For recent and helpful discussion on the nature of the Bible as Scripture, see Craig D. Allert, *A High View of Scripture?* (Grand Rapids: Baker, 2007).

8. On the Bible as text that is has dramatic *effects* on people see J. David Hester, "The Wuellnerian Sublime: Rhetorics, Power and the Ethics of Communi(ca)tion" in *Rhetorics and Hermeneutics: Wilhelm Wuellner and His Influence*, ed. James D. Hester and J. David Hester (New York/London: T&T Clark, 2004) 3–22.

work on the basis of a religion of collective and personal individual experience or a religion of biblical revelation.[9]

It is an ethical and interpretive error to read Rom 1:1–32 as containing rules or as being a kind of handbook for Christian behavior. It is a mistake to read the Bible or any part of it as if it was a rule book or a handbook simply to be read and obeyed. The Bible, and Romans 1 in particular, is simply not written like that. The Bible is a fairly lengthy composite book comprised of historical, narrative, legal, poetic, prophetic, wisdom, biographical, epistolary, apocalyptic, theological documents. In some cases these genres are mixed in complex ways within a single document. Each document must be read (first) for what it actually is, on its own terms. Romans is a letter from Paul the Apostle to the church in Rome. In general, Christians must enter the biblical story, the world and worldview of the biblical canon, and they must not just look for and argue about morality or moral rules. It follows that they must learn to read and actually read the biblical texts carefully and systematically.[10] To do this I will focus on two things: ideology and argumentation.

Romans 1 is ideological and argumentative.[11] That is to say that Paul, the author, wrote (or, more correctly, *spoke*)[12] the Letter to the Romans from a point of view, a worldview, from an understanding of reality that he believed that his audience in Rome shared with him and understood, and he presented an argument, a reasoned and logical case, that aimed to make a point (or multiple points).[13] His ideology and argumentation, however, are crucially important not only because of what they are, but because of what Paul was doing and what he was aiming to achieve ideologically and argumentatively. Paul not only had a multi-

---

9. Here see particularly Markus Bockmuehl, *Seeing the Word: Refocusing New Testament Study* (Grand Rapids: Baker, 2006) especially 146–51.

10. By "systematically" I do not mean according to systematic or dogmatic theological categories, but in a way that reflects the nature and content of the documents and how they are presented in the Bible.

11. As, in fact, are all (biblical) texts and ideas and theologies.

12. Paul was dictating this letter aloud to an amanuensis or dictation secretary, probably Tertius (16:22), rather than writing the words down himself.

13. On ideology and argumentation in the NT, see the particularly helpful approach of Vernon K. Robbins, *Exploring the Textures of Texts: A Guide to Socio-Rhetorical Interpretation* (Harrisburg: Trinity, 1996) 95–119 (ideology) and 21–29 (argumentation). See also L. Gregory Bloomquist, "Paul's Inclusive Language: The Ideological Texture of Romans 1" in *Fabrics of Discourse: Essays in Honor of Vernon K. Robbins*, ed. David B. Gowler, L. Gregory Bloomquist, and Duane F. Watson (Harrisburg: Trinity, 2003) 165–93, particularly 171–76.

faceted ideology, his language aimed at creating ideology. Paul's letters, and, indeed, all of the biblical documents, are not value neutral or ideologically neutral,[14] nor can they ever be imagined or interpreted to be so. Paul's letters—Romans in particular—must therefore be examined not only from the usual historical (i.e., historical-critical) perspective. Historical interpretation is not a guarantee of interpretive accuracy.[15] The letters are living, rhetorical documents that are meant to have and do have ideological and argumentative power and outcomes. They *do* things to people. "Texts do not just evidence preexisting worlds; they create them."[16] Paul was both working from an ideology and, simultaneously, writing his letter to move people toward an ideology, to take a point of view, to come to a particular mindset, to understand and believe in and practice and be strengthened in particular beliefs and behaviors. Ideology and argumentation use *power*, that is, the power of words and language, to get people to think and act in *particular* ways. Paul was aiming, therefore, to be *socially formative*.[17]

IDEOLOGY

Ideology is to be found in the "rhetorical goal" that texts aim to achieve among their readers. This is the goal of creating a conscious "world" where audiences are affected by the text and are moved or persuaded to think and behave in accord with the created "world." The locus of this ideology is in the social, cultural and religious location of the author.[18] Examination aims to come to an understanding of the ideology of the speaker/author, of the ideology shared between speaker/author and audience, and the ideology evoked by the text and how the ideology brings about change.

Paul's ideology is *gospel* ideology. He lives his life in gospel space.[19] The repetitions of the word "gospel" as a noun (*euangelion*, Rom 1:1, 9, 16), by pronouns (1:2, 16, 17), and by the cognate verb (*euangelizō*, 1:15)

---

14. Much less theologically neutral.

15. On this see Dale B. Martin, *Sex and the Single Savior* (Louisville: Westminster John Knox, 2006) 17–35.

16. Bloomquist, "Paul's Inclusive Language," 176.

17. Hence the term "Social Direction" in the title of this essay.

18. See Robbins, *Exploring*, 111.

19. The notion of "space" is taken from Critical Spatiality Theory. Humans inhabit spaces and use language that is reflected in the modes of action and speech and the ideologies that they employ.

make this stand out boldly. His eager rhetoric for the proclamation of it among Gentile peoples (1:14–15) indicates that it is central to, indeed it dominates, his thinking and activity.[20] He sees himself as "having been set apart" for the gospel (1:1). The foundation and presupposition of this gospel is resurrection, the resurrection of Jesus who, Paul was convinced, was thereby marked off as Christ, the Son of God, our Lord (1:4). This raised Jesus is the foundation of Paul's proclamation to Gentile peoples (1:5). Paul believes that this gospel is God's power for the salvation of humans and that it reveals God to be righteous (1:16–17). This gospel ideology, then, functions because of the apocalyptic action of God in raising the dead Jesus. This is what Paul was convinced is true and is what drove him in his apostolic, proclamatory work, and in his writing of letters. Paul believed in resurrection and the gospel as the objective foundation and driver of all that he did. He conformed his life to the gospel, considered it to be the most important and central thing not only in his own life, but in human history and human existence. His letters must be read in light of this ideology. It is neither left, right, nor center; that is, Paul is not interested in artificial politics,[21] but in commitment to the gospel regardless of varying views. His gospel, resurrection ideology is a trajectory that runs in a direction that is dramatically different than how people usually think and how the world and its cultures and its politics typically operate. If Jesus is raised, then everything is different. God has acted in the world to bring about a new situation where people are called to be saints (1:7).

Paul's ideology is *Jewish* ideology. He is a believer in the raised Jesus, but he also inhabits Jewish space. His Jewish ideology is made clear in Romans 1 through his connection of the gospel and Jesus Christ with the promises of God through the prophets in the Holy Scriptures (1:2), with Jesus as a physical descendant of King David (*kata sarka*, 1:3), by the repetitive use of the term "Gentile" (*ethnos*, 1:5–6, 13, 14–15, 16), and by his description of the Gentile condition (1:18–32).[22] Paul is consciously

20. Paul has been so active in preaching the "gospel" that he has been prevented from coming to preach in Rome before the time of writing. His eagerness for the gospel is graphic in the text (1:14–15). This visuality is now being called "rhetography" by socio-rhetorical interpreters; see, for example, Roy R. Jeal, "Clothes Make the (Wo)Man," *Scriptura* 90 (2005) 685–99; "Blending Two Arts: Rhetorical Words, Rhetorical Pictures and Social Formation in the Letter to Philemon," *Sino-Christian Studies* 5 (2008) 9–38.

21. Which is not to say that he does not argue politically or take political positions.

22. The entire section, 1:18–32, is to be understood as a description of Gentiles and assumes Paul's Jewish ideology.

addressing a church in Rome comprised mostly of Gentiles (as 1:13 indicates), and "Greeks and barbarians" (and the "wise and foolish") are the focus of his proclamation of the gospel (1:14–15). But he does work out of Jewish space, recognizing that the gospel is "to Jew first" (1:16), and he assumes that his audience is reasonably acquainted with Jewish Scripture and Jewish traditions (1:2–3, 16). From a Jewish point of view like Paul's, it is the Gentiles, those presumed not to be the elect of God, who fit the description of the ungodly and wicked people who suppress the truth depicted in 1:18–32. For Paul, there is an ideological continuum of Judaism and Christian faith (cf. Rom 10:4).[23] The ancient, holy narrative of Abraham and of Israel, of covenant and promise, of evil and oppression and salvation and freedom, of the prophetic expectation of the Messiah and of God's kingdom, of redemption and the forgiveness of sins and of good for all people, and of the community of the redeemed people (cf. Romans 9–11) is the heart of his worldview. He did not envision a bifurcation with separate Jewish and Christian religions, often hostile toward each other, as has historically been the case, nor did he envision separate ideological narratives. His Jewish ideology places a natural coloring on what he says. Since Paul is ideologically Jewish, he has a Jewish moral/behavioral point of view that is reflected in his description of the moral and behavioral situation of Gentiles in 1:18–32.[24]

Paul's ideology is *ecclesiological* ideology. Paul inhabits the Church, he is a member of the Church and a proclaimer of the gospel of the Church. These things are also true of the audience of Romans, and Paul is very conscious of them in their ecclesiological space. He addresses all those in Rome called saints (1:7) and greets them with his usual wish for grace and peace. This church he knows to be a faithful church (1:8). He wants and intends to visit the church in order to strengthen it and to be strengthened himself by its members (1:11–12), and he wants to preach the gospel in Rome (1:15). Paul's ideology as he speaks this letter is aimed at the church in Rome in order to shape it in particular ways that accord with the gospel, with resurrection and behavior appropriate to these things. Paul's ideology of the Church recognizes the Church's formation as the people of the eschatological Christ in whom God has acted apoca-

---

23. Paul has not rejected basic Jewish notions such as monotheism, election, Torah, and Temple. He has been moved to alter his views, but not to reject them.

24. Though it is critically important, as we shall see, that Paul does not leave Jews out of his behavioral condemnation, in Romans 2 and 3.

lyptically for their benefit, yet he also recognizes that the Church lives in the present and faces people wherever they are, as people for whom Christ died. Paul's ecclesiological ideology recognizes that the Church faces many pressures, but he envisions the Church being strengthened in the gospel.

Paul's ideology is *apostolic* and *prophetic* ideology. Paul dwells in apostolic space, functioning as one who has a commission from Jesus to proclaim the gospel to the Gentiles (1:1; cf. 11:13; 15:20–21). He therefore works from an ideologically authoritative position that allows him not only to address the church in Rome, but to make requests of them.[25] At the same moment, Paul is situated in prophetic space, that is, in the space of proclamation. He is a preacher, in effect a spokesperson for God, a proclaimer of God's word, as 1:13–15 (cf. particularly 10:8 and 15:18) make clear.

Paul's ideology is *truth-seeking*. Paul believes (as will be discussed at more length below) that humans actually know truth and that they engage in suppression of it (1:18–20; 2:1). He is ideologically committed to the notion that truth is real and that it can be and is understood. He does not, contra postmodernist interpretive thought, believe that truth is a social construct or is subjective. Nor, alternatively, does he think that truth is in principle absolute, but unknowable. He does not move outside of the realm that understands that God and truth are both real and knowable things, however difficult they may be to understand and regardless of how many impediments may be in the way of understanding them.[26] Consequently, he thinks that humans are responsible *for* and *to* what they know. Because they reject what they know, God hands them over to negative behaviors (1:24, 26, 28).

Paul is clearly the dominant character in Romans 1 and 2 and, indeed, in the entire letter. He aims to move people to take (or be reminded of) a social and believing, theological position. He draws his audience into agreement by a rhetorical argument that directs readers into the ideological, social, and moral space that he is sure accords with the raised Jesus Christ. This is a space where the gospel and faithfulness

---

25. As Rom 15:23–24, where it is apparent that he plans to ask the Roman church to support him financially for his proposed travels to Spain.

26. For an interesting related discussion, see Errol Morris, "Reply to Comment No. 57, 'The Hooded Man,' The Claim that Postmodernism Should be Given a Chance," *The New York Times*, December 10, 2007. Online: http://morris.blogs.nytimes.com/2007/12/10/primae-objectiones-et-responsio-auctoris-ad-primas-objectiones-part-one.

to it is far more important than humans' situations, than their concerns for themselves, or than their desires and proclivities. His ideologies are political ideologies because they stand against human activities that are not in alignment with them.

ARGUMENTATION

Paul has set out his foundational gospel ideology in the famous words of 1:16–17:

> For I am not ashamed of the gospel; it is the power of God for salvation to everyone who has faith, to the Jew first and also to the Greek. For in it the righteousness of God is revealed through faith for faith; as it is written, "The one who is righteous will live by faith."

From this statement, with its declaration that the righteousness of God is revealed in the gospel, Paul begins a very complex argument that indicates why God's righteous "wrath"[27] is revealed against humans (1:18—3:20). This argument shows that humans, regardless of who they are, regardless of their ethnic and religious backgrounds (Gentiles or Jews), regardless of their social views or of their theological understandings, and regardless of any and all good (or moral or religious) activities they perform, are not themselves righteous, and they live under righteous judgment. There are a number of argumentative textures within this larger presentation. The rhetorical purpose of this argumentation is to make an ideological case for the need for God's grace and mercy on humans, and as a foundation on which to describe how that grace/gospel functions and what God brings about by it.

The overall argument of the entire section (1:18–32 followed by 2:1—3:20) moves forcefully to make a dramatic rhetorical point. In the first major step (1:18–32, the primary focus of our concern here), Paul points out that Gentiles, who are observed particularly by those who are the elect people of God, (i.e., Jews),[28] stand without excuse for their failures to honor God. God is not only knowable, but his existence, according

---

27. The word "wrath" (*orgē*) does not refer to the emotion of anger, but to the appropriate and righteous response to what humans have done. Cf. Bloomquist, "Paul's Inclusive Language," 180–81.

28. There are Jewish Christians in Paul's church audience in Rome, as Rom 3:2, 9, 17–24, seen together, indicate.

to Paul, is clear by virtue of the existence and orderliness of the created order, the universe:

> Ever since the creation of the world his eternal power and divine nature, invisible (*unseen*) though they are, have been understood and seen through the things he has made. So they are without excuse. (1:20)

This basic human knowledge has been rejected:

> ... they did not honor him as God or give thanks to him. (1:21a)

This rejection is the real issue for humans, for the Gentiles, that Paul, so far, has in view in his narration. Gentile humans ignore and dishonor God, even though they know that God must exist and that they are responsible to God. It is not the acceptance of God, but the rejection of God, of the knowledge of God, that is the human problem. The rejection of clear and properly informed knowledge progresses to a reshaping of thinking toward idolatry:

> ... but they became futile in their thinking, and their senseless minds were darkened. Claiming to be wise, they became fools; and they exchanged the glory of the immortal God for images resembling a mortal human being or birds or four-footed animals or reptiles. (1:21b–23)

From a Jewish ideological point of view this progression is an unfaithful, if typically and horrifyingly Gentile, outcome (cf. Deut 4:15–20). Paul here reconfigures the ideas found in Wisdom of Solomon 12–14, where the Gentile error of willful idolatry is described in detail.[29] Due to this willful rejection of proper knowledge, God "handed them over in the desires of their hearts" (1:24). This "handing over" (or delivering; committing; *paradidōmi*), repeated three times (1:24, 26, 28), is, in the argument, the righteous action of the righteous God. It is critically important to understand, however, that God hands the Gentile rejecters of the proper honor and thanksgiving of God over to *behaviors*. The behaviors to which God delivers them are the result, the penalty, of the rejection of the clear knowledge of God. This is a critical point because it is frequently misconstrued: condemnation is not the result of the behaviors described in

---

29. See Bloomquist, "Paul's Inclusive Language," 182–84. The extra-canonical Wisdom was quite clearly known by Paul, and its ideas, and perhaps the document itself, were known to Jewish believers.

1:24–32, rather the behaviors are the result of the condemnation, of God delivering people to the behaviors. The behaviors are not a *cause*, but a *result*, the result of ignoring, dishonoring, and failing to thank God and by exchanging God for non-god(s). The underlying problem, however, is not idolatry, is not the choice of idolatry or of a particular idol. The problem is not about vice, but about "unfaith," about the willful rejection of God, the rejection of trust in God, who is known to be present. The upshot of this unfaith is idolatry.[30] The step between rejection and idolatry is an easy, probably inevitable step, which springs out of the refusal to adhere to correct knowledge.

The argument, so far, can be laid out helpfully as follows:

> *Rule*: people (Gentiles) know that there is God. Their knowledge informs them that they are responsible to this knowledge and to God and they have no excuse for not aligning themselves with this knowledge (i.e., by honoring and giving thanks to God).
>
> *Case*: people having this knowledge nevertheless ignore God and fail to thank God.
>
> *Result*: they exchange the knowledge of God for non-gods, substitute gods, and are given over by God to wrong behaviors.

Having made his argument thus far, Paul moves ahead by drawing the Jewish Christian members of his audience directly into the argument (2:1–11). In fact, Paul has laid a subtle trap for those, particularly Jewish Christians, who find themselves agreeing, nodding their heads with what he has said in 1:18–32. They agree that those people, Gentiles who live apart from the monotheistic, elect, Torah-abiding community, practice the idolatry and behaviors Paul has just described. They are moved, rhetorically, now to participate, apparently with Paul, who is also a Jewish Christian and seems to have a clear Jewish point of view, in condemning such people. They are happy to say, as Paul visualizes and hears them as he speaks, that "We know that God's judgment on those who do such things is in accordance with truth" (2:2). They recognize, judge, and disparage people whom they perceive to be particularly odious. At this moment Paul's trap springs, and they are inescapably caught up in it. Paul slices their self-righteous and self-congratulatory judgment and attitude to shreds because he points out what should be as obvious as

---

30. This is important because Paul is not saying that homoerotic and other activities are *based* in idolatry, and it does not follow that homosexuality would disappear if idolatry disappeared. Cf. Martin, *Sex and the Single Savior*, 55.

the Gentile rejection of the knowledge of God: they do the same things. They are, therefore, like those whom they judge, without excuse (2:1–11). Election does not spare anyone from condemnation. They have no legs to stand on. They are in exactly the same condition and under the same judgments as those whom they cheerfully disparage. Paul goes on from this point in his argument to stark and unavoidable conclusions:

> ... we have already charged that all, both Jews and Greeks, are under the power of sin, as it is written: "There is no one who is righteous, not even one." (3:9–10)

> Now we know that whatever the law says, it speaks to those who are under the law, so that every mouth may be silenced, and the whole world may be held accountable to God. For "no human being will be justified in his sight" by deeds prescribed by the law, for through the law comes the knowledge of sin. (3:19–20)

> ... since all have sinned and fall short of the glory of God. (3:23)

No amount of good behavior or of following the rules or observing laws or the law will help.[31] Humans, all of them, all of us, whether Jews or Gentiles, are simply guilty. There is no appeal, there is no making up for bad decisions, bad behaviors, or mistakes. We are fairly and righteously judged. Paul's point is quite clear. It can be set out like this:

> *Case*: Gentiles, the people of the world, do not honour and thank God as they know they should. They exchange the knowledge of God for non-gods, for substitute gods, and are given over by God to wrong behaviors. Those who see themselves as the chosen/elect of God (Jews) look at it and shake their heads—it is so awful, sordid, ungodly—and agree that it is right for those people of the world to be judged and condemned by God.

> *Rationale*: those who piously agree that the sinners should be judged practice the same things.[32] They stand, therefore, equally

---

31. Morris, in *The New York Times*, refers to an article he read in *The New York Review of Books* about a German physician who had been charged for conducting medical experiments on children during the Third Reich. For his defense the physician claimed "... but I've lived an exemplary life, if you don't include the tuberculosis experiments I performed on children." Exemplary life indeed (if there really is such a thing) but that does not remove the guilt of one bad deed. Going through a stop sign is not corrected by stopping twice at the next one.

32. As this is being written, the news about (former) Governor Spitzer of New York is attracting attention. Spitzer took a strong moral stand and prosecuted prostitution rings, yet is himself alleged to have employed prostitutes.

subject to judgment and condemnation (2:4). God is not partial, does not show favorites (2:11).[33]

Result: everyone is judged and condemned. There is no escape, there is nothing anyone can do, guilt is universal. This is simply how it is for humans. No one can now be "good enough" to avoid or overcome or abolish judgment.

The good news, of course, is that God loves (us) all anyway, and Christ has been faithful for us in the shedding of his blood (3:21–26).

In this argumentation, Paul demonstrates clearly, though he comes to it subtly, that individuals or groups of persons must hesitate *to judge and condemn* other individuals or groups for their knowing rejection of truth since they themselves are already guilty of the same kinds of actions. At the same time, Paul neither justifies nor accepts the wrong behaviors, nor does he allow for their intentional, continued practice. Indeed he calls for all believers to take on his ideological position that sets the gospel and faithfulness to it at the center of life, to live in gospel space, *regardless of what may need to be given up for its sake* (cf. Rom 6; Phil 3; 1 Cor 9). Sinners are not rejected,[34] but they are called to refuse the sin.

Internally, the large block of argument contains the focused statements of 1:24–27 that are of particular interest:

Therefore God gave them up in the lusts of their hearts to impurity, to the degrading of their bodies among themselves, because they exchanged the truth about God for a lie and worshiped and served the creature rather than the Creator, who is blessed forever! Amen. For this reason God gave them up to dishonoring passions. Their women exchanged natural intercourse for unnatural, and in the same way also the men, giving up natural intercourse with women, were consumed with passion for one another. Men committed shameless acts with men and received in their own persons the due penalty for their error.

Among the behaviors to which God has delivered people are the "dishonoring" (*atimazō*, in NRSV "degrading") of their own bodies. Paul calls this being given over "in the lusts of their hearts into uncleanness of the dishonoring of their bodies among themselves." Bodies are very impor-

---

33. Judgment cuts both ways. Those who condemn people who judge other people are themselves judged for their condemnation of others. On this, see Rom 14:1–15:13.

34. They are indeed *loved* (Rom 5:6–10).

tant things to Paul. His Jewish and gospel ideology integrates physiology and physicality with behavior.[35] Bodies are also important to Jesus, who healed them, gave them sight and mobility, removed demons from them, fed them, and calmed storms for them.[36] For Paul, human lives are lived in bodies,[37] and the ways in which bodies are used are important and should reflect the gospel and gospel ideology. This ideological view becomes narrowly framed and specific in 1:26–27 where Paul states that God delivers people over to "dishonoring passions." These are specified as homoerotic activities by both females and males that are designated as an exchange of natural function into function against (or beside[38]) nature (*para physin*). Paul states that "males" in particular (*arsenes*) are "inflamed in their desire for one another," "male in male" with these "shameless acts" "producing the response" "necessary" to be "received from their wandering."[39]

It is important to point out that the language Paul uses does not refer directly to pederasty (i.e., sexual activity between an adult male and a boy) though it includes it, nor does it refer solely to the homoerotic sexual activity of a heterosexual person, where this behavior could be seen to be "against nature" or "unnatural," that is, against nature for that specific person. Paul refers, rather, to homosexual acts in general, whether of females or males, not to specified activities.[40] Whatever one thinks of Paul as a person or as an apostle and preacher and pastor, it is specious to claim, as some have, that he approved of, or would have approved of, homosexual activities.[41] The "shameless acts" are actual

---

35. Cf. 1 Thess 5:23, "May the God of peace himself sanctify you *entirely*; and may your *spirit* and *soul* and *body* be kept sound and blameless at the coming of our Lord Jesus Christ."

36. The separation of body and soul or body and spirit is not a biblical or Christian notion. The NT does not separate the spiritual from the physical.

37. Cf. 2 Cor 5:1-5; 1 Cor 15:35-58.

38. Martin claims that *para physin* should here be understood to mean "beyond nature" (Martin, *Sex and the Single Savior*, 54, 57).

39. My translation of specific words to convey Paul's Greek.

40. Some ancient moralists considered homosexual activity to be "the most extreme expression of heterosexual lust" (V. P. Furnish quoted in Martin, *Sex and the Single Savior*, 57).

41. As Martin, *Sex and the Single Savior*, 51, points out. For the claim that Paul was supportive, see John Boswell, *Christianity, Social Tolerance, and Homosexuality: Gay People in Western Europe From the Beginning of the Christian Era until the Fourteenth Century* (Chicago: University of Chicago Press, 1980). Others claim that Paul did not view same-sex relations as sin, but as part of the "dirtiness" into which Gentile people had been committed by God. On this, see L. William Countryman, *Dirt, Greed and Sex:*

sexual activities—not, it must be stated, the inclination toward or the desire for such activities, but the acts themselves.[42] Paul does not, as Dale B. Martin points out, offer a clear etiology of homosexual desire, and we should not think that he would be concerned to provide one.[43] But he does think homosexual activity is unrighteous and that, however desirable it may be to some people, it does not accord with behavior that honors (gives glory, *doxazō*) to God.

Homosexual activity was certainly well-known and widely practiced in the ancient Mediterranean basin.[44] Paul of course knew this. Sometimes it was quite highly regarded.[45] In Judaism, however, it was considered to be activity out of accord with the created order set in place by God. It was, therefore, considered to be activity that was other than the fullness of life intended by God.[46] Paul does not make a long and full argument about it—he is, after all, writing a *letter* that is focused on other topics[47]—but relies on his audience(s) to track his overall argument in order to get the point. Directly stated, he takes the ideological, historical, Jewish and, because it not only springs out of Judaism but is the logical continuum of Judaism and belief in Yahweh, the Christian view that homosexual activity is against the way things are intended to be for humans.

Paul is not, in his argumentation in Romans 1, saying that people, Christians in particular, cannot engage in homosexual activity. They can. They can do whatever they like. His argumentation does claim, however, that some things, including homoerotic activity, are unrighteous behaviors. In Rom 1:18–32 Paul is not claiming that some behaviors incur more or stronger consequences than others. Homosexual behavior does not

---

Sexual Ethics in the New Testament and their Implications for Today (Philadelphia: Fortress, 1988).

42. Nor is Paul concerned here about "gender domination," as Jack Rogers, *Jesus, the Bible, and Homosexuality* (Louisville: Westminster John Knox, 2006) 78, claims.

43. See Martin, *Sex and the Single Savior*, 56–60. Whether Paul and various of his interpreters are aiming to preserve a heterosexist, male-female hierarchy, as Martin claims, is debatable.

44. I am conscious that the categorizing terms "homosexual" and "homosexuality" are modern coinings, perhaps dating from as recently as the 1890s.

45. See the references in J. D. G. Dunn, *Romans 1–8*, Word Biblical Commentary Series 38A (Dallas: Word, 1988) 65.

46. See N. T. Wright, "Romans" (*New Interpreter's Bible* Vol X, Nashville: Abingdon, 2002) 430.

47. Homosexuality was not a big item in the early church. Neither church nor sociocultural situations made it a point of concern like it is in our own time.

need to be seen as more egregious than anything else. His argumentation is designed to lead people to the conclusion that all are guilty.

Certainly not everyone shares Paul's view.[48] Many people do not agree that homoerotic activities are "against nature." Many argue that homosexuality is altogether natural, is genetic, and is something some people are born with. Paul only here in his letters takes up his views about what is "according to" or "against" nature in regard to sexual behaviors.[49] His argumentation comes out of his gospel ideology, informed as it is by his Jewish ideology. He argues it as being ecclesiological ideology, and believes his church audience will agree with him. To say that Paul is mistaken is to stand against him ideologically and argumentatively. It is also to say that Scripture is not really or not fully—perhaps not even—a true and trustworthy guide.

SOCIAL DIRECTION

Paul clearly does work from a worldview or understanding of reality. He was, as apostle and prophet, aiming to create a Christian worldview and a Christian social direction. In Romans 1 (and up to 3:20) Paul is creating a social understanding of the human condition. All humans are guilty before God. They all deserve the same penalty, *viz.* death (1:32). No humans can extract themselves from either the guilt or from the penalty for the guilt. Paul's language rhetorically and implicitly aims to move and does move his implied readers to agree with him, to nod their heads in assent. Paul does not believe nor does he suggest that what he says is a social construct or simply a Judeo-Christian way of saying things, apart from actual reality. He is convinced that what he says is true and real. He believes in revealed truth and in the reality of Jesus's resurrection. This is unavoidable in Paul. Resurrection supports, presupposes, every view. He presents a rhetorical argument that directs his audiences toward the social and moral space that he is sure accords with the raised Jesus Christ. This is a space where the gospel and faithfulness to it are far more important than humans' situations, than their concerns for themselves, or than their desires and proclivities. This is the space and the faith of all generations of Christians and of the Church. To deny it or to set it aside is, frankly, to deviate from what Paul believed and taught. Paul's words, though, do indicate some particular features of social direction.

48. Cf. Martin, *Sex and the Single Savior*, 55.
49. Although he certainly mentions sexuality in a number of places.

First, Paul recognizes people as human beings. This is clearly where Romans is leading its audiences (cf. 2 Cor 5:16). That is, he recognizes humans in their humanity as people who reject knowledge they are aware is good and true, and that they even violate what they know. They may engage in behaviors that are deleterious to themselves and to others, and may be repugnant to some. They stand under judgment. So do we. This does not turn Paul away from people; in fact it encourages him to preach all the more, so that God's good news will be heard and understood by them. Rather than divided from people, much less denouncing people, including those who practice any of the behaviors to which he says God delivers them, he wants them to be included. Helpful here is the following quotation from Vancouver physician Gabor Maté's recent book *In the Realm of Hungry Ghosts*. Maté works with drug addicts, the poor and the marginalized in Vancouver's notorious Downtown Eastside:

> At heart, I'm not different from my patients, and sometimes I cannot stand seeing what little psychic space, what little heaven-granted grace, separates me from them. . . . There are moments when I'm revolted by my patients disheveled appearance, their stained and decayed teeth, the look of insatiable hunger in their eyes, their demands, complaints and neediness. Those are times when I would do well to examine myself for irresponsibility in my own life, for self-neglect—in my case not so much physical but spiritual—and for placing false needs above real ones.
>
> When I am sharply judgmental of any other person, it's because I sense or see reflected in them some aspect of myself that I don't want to acknowledge. I'm speaking here of not of my *critique* of another person's behavior in objective terms but of the self-righteous tone of personal *judgment* that colours my opinion. If, for example, I resent some person close to me as "controlling," it may be owing to my own inability to assert myself. Or I may react against another person because she has a trait that I myself have—and dislike, but don't wish to acknowledge: for example a tendency to want to control others. . . . some mornings I vituperate about right-wing political columnists. My opinion remains more or less constant: their views are based on a highly selective reading of the facts and rooted in a denial of reality. What does vary from day to day is the emotional charge that infuses my opinion. Some days I dismiss them with intense hostility; at other times I see their perspective as one possible way of looking at things.

> On the surface, the differences are obvious.... Moral judgments, however, are never about the obvious; they always speak to the underlying similarities between the judge and the condemned. My judgments of others are an accurate gauge of how, beneath the surface, I feel about myself. It's only the willful blindness in me that condemns another for deluding himself; my own selfishness that excoriates another for being self-serving; my lack of authenticity that judges falsehood in another.[50]

This reflects Paul's description of the human condition in Romans 1–2. It is not for us to condemn those whom God has already condemned. Paul quite clearly includes those who engage in homoerotic activities among them. To condemn would be to fall into the trap Paul springs in 2:1–4 and to be caught in our own argument due to our own behaviors. But, this refusal to condemn *does not mean* that homoerotic behavior or any of the behaviors Paul mentions in 1:28–32 are to be *approved*. Paul clearly does not approve of them or bless them in any way.

Second, Paul understands that the gospel itself calls people to faith and faithfulness. This is at the heart of what Paul addresses in Romans 1 (and in the entire letter). Already in 1:17 he stated that "the one who is righteous will live by faith" (more literally, "the righteous person will live out of faith," a reconfiguration of LXX Hab 2:4). This faith recognizes the deep truth of the gospel of the raised Jesus Christ and shapes life to align with it. For Paul this means giving up one's rights, abilities, interests, and proclivities for the gospel's sake. The gospel makes a prior claim on Christians for faithful living, not for the fulfillment of individual rights and self-determination. The social tendency to personal independence sometimes stands against faithfulness to the gospel at the expense of healthy self-denial. When behavior is questionable or its moral ground subject to debate, it should follow the faith indicated in scripture. Nothing is more important than Christ and the gospel. For Paul it is worth the loss of everything, including one's sexuality and self-determination and personal needs. What Paul does not call for is the simple *replacement* of what he considers wrong behavior by right behavior. Virtue is not the opposite of vice; faith is the opposite of vice. The calling of the gospel to faith and behavior requires, of course, an actual return to preaching the gospel and to the ideology of the gospel, something that has frequently been, in my view at least, forgotten or lost.

50. Gabor Maté, *In the Realm of Hungry Ghosts* (Toronto: Knopf Canada, 2008) 253–54.

CONCLUSION

Romans 1, taken as the foundational New Testament text addressing homoerotic activity, argues that same-sex intercourse is behavior to which God has delivered some people and that it is not righteous activity of faith. Well-intentioned alternative interpretations do not stand up to scrutiny. Paul was ideologically focused on the gospel and was not likely to be persuaded by concerns for social situations and social correctness or by concerns for individual rights. What does this say about homosexuality and the church?

It pushes us to conclude that persons who engage in homosexual behavior—gays, lesbians or heterosexuals—are, *like all of us*, people who have failed to honor and thank God, who is known to us. No one is better than anyone else, Jew or Gentile, gay or straight. Paul calls us to accept this fact. We may not disparage or hate anyone or fail to respect anyone on either side of the current debates. People are to be respected where they are and wherever they have come from. We must, I think obviously, avoid the worn statements like "love the sinner but hate the sin" because they are trite and platitudinous, but also because they are patronizing of what many people think is right and correct for them. We must be conscious that we live in a pluralistic, tolerant, and highly individualistic society. We may not, however, taking Paul seriously and authoritatively, take the view that homosexual activity is righteous behavior. It is clear that Scripture allows that homosexual activity occurs; but it neither authorizes nor supports it. In fact it calls us to abstain from it.

Paul is not giving commands or orders in Romans 1; he is explaining the human condition and setting a trajectory for social direction for the Church. He assumes that his point in 1:18—3:20 is made and that his readers get the idea and that they will agree. The point for Paul was not about personal freedom to do things, but doing things so that proclamation of Christ could be made for the sake of the salvation of others. A major question for us is whether Paul's words are taken to have apostolic authority or as merely a reflection of his own social and religious views. Paul believed in revelation in the form of resurrection (cf. Gal 1:11–24). On this gospel ideology he took his stand, proclaimed his message, and called for Christians everywhere to believe and behave accordingly.

3

Friendship

The End of Marriage

Gary Thorne

This article is intended to contribute to the debate about whether the Church should perform wedding ceremonies for two persons of the same sex, or bless such weddings performed by civil authorities. I begin with an assumption that I shall maintain throughout, that the quality and depth of love between two men or two women can be as deep and profound as the love experienced between two persons of opposite sex. Two men or two women can be struck by Cupid's arrow in much the same way as a man and a woman, and have similar experiences of "falling in love" with one another. In the tradition of the Church, when a Christian man and woman discover themselves to be "in love," often this couple will prayerfully seek discernment about whether it is God's will for them to live together for the rest of their lives in a marriage established by the exchange of vows of mutual fidelity to "love and to cherish, till death do us part." The tradition of the Church has never formally allowed a man and man or woman and woman couple who find themselves "in love" to take these vows. Many argue that the time has come for the Church to offer marriage as an option for same sex couples.

But what does this have to do with friendship? Friendship-love at first might seem to be something very different from the "romantic" or erotic love of marriage. In this essay I shall suggest that erotic love (along with *philia* love and *agapē* love) is present in many types of friendship-love, whether that friendship-love is found inside or outside of marriage. Indeed, I believe that the Church has inadequately understood friendship-love in recent times and that this lack of understanding has contributed to a confusion in the Church about the relationship of friendship-love and marriage. In my pastoral ministry of twenty-five years, I have many times felt handicapped by the shallow valuation given to "friendship" in Christian discourse. In my experience "friendship" is seldom acknowledged as including the possibility of particular relationships of profound intimacy, spiritual union, and mutual "exchange." Rather, friendship is considered to be a less intimate and inferior form of relationship than that found in marriage. Thus the same-sex "covenanted friendship" in the Christian tradition, described most recently by authors such as Pavel Florensky, John Boswell, and Alan Bray, is almost always immediately equated with marriage, or a parody of marriage, rather than seen as a distinct and profound instance of friendship. I hope that this essay will contribute in some way toward restoring confidence in the divine beauty and eternal character of friendship. My overall conclusion is that a recovery of a fuller Christian appreciation of friendship and friendship-love is urgently needed in our present debate.

It is difficult to begin with a definition of friendship because there are many different types of friendship. Nevertheless, I suggest that most people today might think of friendship as a particular relationship or activity of mutual and reciprocal goodwill, characterized by qualities of honesty, trust, respect, self-disclosure, caring, and affection, between people who seek to spend time together. Cicero defines friendship as "agreement in all things divine and human, with benevolence and charity" (*De Amicitia* 6.20). Both these definitions—modern and ancient—serve to distance our discussion of friendship from the two types of friendship that Aristotle says are only friendships "incidentally"—*viz.* friendships of pleasure or friendships of usefulness (*Nichomachean Ethics* 1156a). Finally, within the broad spectrum of human friendships, we will be considering only those friendships that have a "lasting," "life-long," or even "eternal" character.

For the past four hundred years or so there has been very little philosophical consideration of friendship as an essential force in the shaping of culture, moral life, and human happiness. Writing in the 1950s, C. S.

Lewis remarks on the lack of attention given to the subject of friendship in modern times:

> To the Ancients, Friendship seemed the happiest and most fully human of all loves; the crown of life and the school of virtue. The modern world, in comparison, ignores it.... If a man believes (as I do) that the old estimate of friendship was the correct one, he can hardly write a chapter on it except as rehabilitation.[1]

I begin my consideration of friendship generally with a remarkable study that appeared in Russia in 1914, though translated into English only in 1997. Its author, Pavel Florensky (1882–1937), a Russian Orthodox priest, was one of the most remarkable polymaths of the twentieth century. His study of friendship is contained in his book *The Pillar and Ground of the Truth*,[2] which takes its theme from 1 Tim 3:15:

> I hope to come to you soon, but I [Paul] am writing these instructions to you [Timothy] so that, if I am delayed, you may know how one ought to behave in the household of God, which is the Church of the living God, the pillar and ground of truth.

Florensky's argument is that in the household of God we are meant to relate to one another as friends, with friendship-love, and only in this way will we know the truth of the Christian faith. In form and style, Florensky's work consists of twelve letters addressed to the reader as if to a friend. The book has been criticized because it does not proceed as a systematic study, but is rather full of digressions, excurses, appendices, and labored footnotes. But Florensky intentionally writes in this manner, as if he was having a conversation over a period of time with a friend. It is in this way, through an encounter in friendship, that the truth of the Christian faith will be known.[3]

---

1. C. S. Lewis, *The Four Loves* (San Diego, New York, London: Geoffrey Bles, 1960) 87, 90.

2. Pavel Florensky, *The Pillar and Ground of the Truth: An Essay in Orthodox Theodicy in Twelve Letters*, trans. and annotated by Boris Jakim (Princeton: Princeton University Press, 1997).

3. This is a traditional mode of expression in Christian theology, reaching back through the genres of *eratopokriseis* (Mark of Ephesus, Michael Glykas, Nicholas of Methone, Psellus, Photius, Maximus the Confessor, Anastasius of Sinai) and *kephalaia* (Gregory Palamas, Maximus the Confessor, Diadochus of Photike, Evagrius Ponticus) all the way to *apophthegmata* and their early transmission via letters (cf. Barsanouphius and John). This style rests on a definite epistemological assertion and an important pedagogic approach. The *Stromateis* (or "Ragbag") of Clement of Alexandria (ca. 150–215) is more or less a collection of jottings in the precise way that Florensky identifies his work (5)—full of themes difficult to sort out and state systematically.

Friendship is the subject of the eleventh letter of the series. He has already revealed to the reader in a previous letter on Holy Sophia that Sophia, Truth, and Friendship are connected. Friendship is required to know Sophia and experience Truth. Only in friendship do we participate in "that spiritual activity in which and by means of which the knowledge of the Pillar of Truth is given."[4] Florensky suggests that in Christianity the most fundamental unit is not the individual man understood as an atomic unit, but rather the pair of friends as the basic molecule. It is a brilliant study in which Florensky mines the intellectual history of East and West, ancients and moderns, Christians, Jews and pagans.

> Philia knows a friend not by his outward pose, not by the dress of heroism, but by his smile, by his quiet talk, by his weaknesses, by how he treats people in ordinary human life, by how he eats and sleeps . . . the true test of a soul's authenticity is through life together, in the love of friends. . . .
>
> What is friendship? Self-contemplation through a friend in God. Friendship is the seeing of oneself with the eyes of another, but before a third, namely, the Third. . . . Friendship gives people self-knowledge. Friendship reveals where and how one must work on oneself.[5]

Drawing upon his masterful familiarity with the classical tradition, Florensky describes friends as mirrors in which we see ourselves, both what is lovely and what needs to be re-arranged in our own souls. *Agapē*-love—that rational willing of the good for all persons—is dependent on a friendship-love (*philia*), and vice versa:

> In order to treat everyone as oneself [*agapē*-love] it is necessary to *see* oneself at least in one person, to feel oneself in him; it is necessary to perceive in this one person an already achieved—even if only partial—victory over selfhood. . . . But for *philia* love of a Friend not to degenerate in a peculiar self-love, for a Friend not to become merely the condition of a comfortable life, for friendship to have a depth, . . . what is necessary is *agapē* love, . . . *philia* is the "leaven," while *agapē* is the "salt" that keeps human relations from spoiling.[6]

---

4. Florensky, *Pillar and Ground of the Truth*, x.
5. Ibid., 314.
6. Ibid., 297.

In his discussion of the four Greek words for love (*eros*; *storgē*; *philia*; *agapē*), Florensky acknowledges that these notions inform one another and are not really four different "things." For example, he uses the word *philia* as relating closest to friendship-love, but insists that *eros* and *agapē* must also be present in the love of friends. He concludes this discussion with a moving meditation on the last chapter of the Gospel of John (21) in which he points to friendship-love as the highest love. In friendship-love, *agapē* is embodied and made real.[7]

Florensky also presents the ancient Christian rites of *adelphopoiesis* (brother-making, or the pledging of brotherhood) in which two males or two females are joined together in a covenant of chaste bonds of friendship-love. He describes a typical expression of the rite as containing the following elements: (1) the brothers stand before the lectern upon which are the Cross and the Gospel; (2) prayers and litanies are said that ask that the two be united in love and that remind them of examples of friendships from church history; (3) the two are tied with one belt, their hands are placed on the Gospel, and a burning candle is given to each of them; (4) readings from Scripture, including John 17:18–26; . . . (7) the brothers partake of the pre-sanctified gifts from a common cup; (8) they are led around the lectern while they hold hands, as the *troparion* is sung ("Lord, watch from heaven and see"); (9) they exchange kisses; and (10) the following is sung: "Behold, how good and how pleasant it is for brethren to dwell together in unity!" (Ps 133:1). The exchange of the cross takes place either before or during the rite, as a sign that the brothers will bear each other's crosses, and as a reminder of self-renunciation and faithfulness to the friend.[8]

Florensky concludes that friendship-love is the highest love, inclusive of *eros* and *agapē* in the divinely ordered particularity of *philia*. In this he truly reflects the philosophy and tradition from Plato and Aristotle through to Aelred of Rievault (twelfth century), Aquinas, and Dante. Unfortunately, however, at the time of the sixteenth-century Reformation this rich understanding of friendship was largely forgotten or intentionally put aside. Friendship began to receive very little philosophical and theological consideration in the West. The reason is, simply, according to Meilaender, that "Within Christian thought *agapē* displaced *philia* [friendship], and it is impossible to think theologically about

---

7. Ibid., 291, 326.
8. Described in ibid., 327, 328.

love without giving that simple fact careful consideration."[9] Luther, for example, refused to allow friendship to have any role in ethics since he interpreted it narrowly as merely a form of self-love. In Anglican circles, Jeremy Taylor (1613-1667) might come to mind as an exception, but in actual fact he did not encourage particular friendships as much as he understood friendship in a universal way, describing the Christian as a friend with all the world. Of particular friendships he writes, ". . . when friendships were the noblest things in the world, charity was little."[10] Further, for Taylor marriage becomes the single particular state of life in which highest friendship finds an appropriate place.

The problem that was identified with friendship or *philia* is that it is an exclusive, preferential, reciprocal love. Jealousy and possessiveness belong to friendship. *Agapē*, on the other hand, is an inclusive, unconditional, universal love, blind to merit or demerit, that goes out to everyone, even to the enemy who will not return such love. Søren Kierkegaard and Anders Nygren remain true to this modern notion that Christian *agapē* must leave the preferential love of friendship behind. In the nineteenth century Kierkegaard wrote:

> Christianity has thrust erotic love and friendship from the throne, the love rooted in mood and inclination, preferential love, in order to establish spiritual love in its place, love to one's neighbor, a love which in all earnestness and truth is inwardly more tender in the union of two persons than erotic love is and more faithful in the sincerity of close relationship than the most famous friendship. . . . the praise of erotic love and friendship belong to paganism. . . . what belongs to Christianity [is] love to one's neighbor, of which not a trace is found in paganism. . . .
>
> In . . . friendship one's neighbor is not loved, but one's otherself. If anyone thinks that . . . by finding a friend he has learned Christian love, he is in profound error.[11]

Nygren's criticism of friendship in the mid-twentieth century is dependent on Kierkegaard's reasoning, but is even more fundamental

---

9. Gilbert Meilaender, *Friendship: A Study in Theological Ethics* (South Bend: University of Notre Dame Press, 1981) 2.

10. Jeremy Taylor, "A Discourse on the Nature and Offices of Friendship" in *The Whole Works of the Right Rev Jeremy Taylor*, vol 1, ed. R. Heber (London: Ogle, Duncan, 1847-1854) 72.

11. Søren Kierkegaard, *Works of Love*, trans. Howard and Edna Hong (New York: Harper & Row, 1964) 58, 68.

in that he recognizes and despairs that St. John, in his Gospel and in his letters, speaks of friendship as divinely sanctioned. In John 15 Jesus speaks of his disciples becoming his friends: "You are my friends if you do as I command you" (15:14). He commands his disciples to be friends, and the specific nature of the love of the new commandment is that his disciples should love one another "as I have loved you" (15:12). This love is of such a quality and nature that it will be recognized by others: ". . . by this all men will know that you are my disciples, if you have love for one another" (John 13:35). The love here is the distinct love of friendship of the new community, which was to be the continuation of his body in the world. Nygren cannot understand how this can square with the *agapē* love he finds in the Synoptics and in Paul. That *agapē* love is described by Nygren as being undeserved, spontaneous, and unmotivated. Johannine friendship-love, on the other hand, is preferential, and thus Nygren concludes that "it loses something of its original, all-embracing scope; it becomes love for those who bear the Christian name."[12]

But the preferential aspect of friendship has not only drawn fire from Christian theologians in the modern world. It has equally created problems for moral philosophy. If friendship is emotional, partial, and personal, then how can it find a place within contemporary ethical theories which are rooted in the Enlightenment notion that moral decisions must be rational, impartial, and universal? In a simplistic manner of speaking it might be said that the Enlightenment project was to "make secular" a particular understanding of the Christian religion in an attempt to form and inform culture itself with Christian principles. Thus, for example, the process of secularization involved the transformation of divine law into the universal rule of rationality; tribalism is overcome and the impartial principle of universal *agapē*-love and the absolute value of and respect for each individual soul becomes incarnated in a principled, enlightened society in which everyone must willingly and freely sacrifice personal desires to the extent that they encroach on the rights of others who also have absolute value. Contemporary Canadian society is profoundly shaped by just such an Enlightenment or "liberal" understanding, which is praised as that which holds our pluralistic nation together. Our social institutions and commitment to such universal moral principles insure cooperation among people who share no common notion of the good or the virtuous life.

---

12. Anders Nygren, *Agape and Eros*, trans. Philip S. Watson (London: SPCK, 1953) 154.

Thus, while the Reformation theologians were championing *agapē*-love over a narrowly understood *philia*-love, the Kantian moral philosophy model established a discipline of ethics in terms of the moral agent as a rational, abstract, solitary individual who makes moral choices by a reflection that removes all particularity. The rational moral agent seeks the universal rule or principle that always applies in this situation or, better still, in all situations. In the Kantian frame, the moral life is that life which is true to a continual reflection upon the question "What would be the duty of any rational being in this particular situation?" Iris Murdoch suggests that much contemporary moral thinking depends on this Kantian view of the individual as,

> rational and totally free.... He is morally speaking monarch of all he surveys and totally responsible for his actions. Nothing transcends him.... We no longer see man against a background of values, of realities which transcend him. We picture man as a brave naked will surrounded by an easily comprehended empirical world. For the hard idea of truth we have substituted a facile idea of sincerity.[13]

Generally speaking, contemporary ethical theories fall under two main headings. There are theories that develop from deontology, which identifies moral reasons for action as those that are universalizable and impartial, and there are theories that develop as instances of consequentialism,[14] according to which a moral agent does whatever action produces the greatest aggregate welfare for all human beings: universal benevolence. In either case, the partiality of friendship on the one hand, and its exclusivity on the other, makes friendship ethically problematic and suspect. As long as these Enlightenment notions of self and ethics were not seriously challenged, there was little interest in the notion of friendship.

The challenge came in the last quarter of the twentieth century when a virtue approach to ethics was promoted directly as the result of a critique of the understanding of the ethical life that has its roots in the Enlightenment. "Virtue ethics" proposes that the central concern of the moral life is the formation of a good and worthy character. The task of

---

13. Iris Murdoch, "Against Dryness: A Polemical Sketch," in *Revisions: Changing Perspectives in Moral Philosophy*, eds. Stanley Hauerwas and Alasdair MacIntyre (South Bend: University of Notre Dame Press, 1983) 44.

14. Utilitarianism can be seen as an instance of consequentialism.

becoming a good person is dependent upon the development of virtues that will help guide us to the good life, happiness (*eudaimonia*, "the best possible life"[15]) or the life worth living. This development and growth in virtue requires relationships with people who share a common vision and desire of the good: our best and closest friends. We cannot acquire the virtues nor flourish in the virtuous life apart from our friendships. First, in our friends, we have a mirror of our souls—we see ourselves in the other and we achieve a continual self-awareness and self-examination that can only come from trusting, open, honest communication and interaction. Second, the friend wishes happiness, "the good and fulfilling life," for her friend, and in so doing becomes herself the person she wishes her friend to become. By seeking happiness or the "life worth living" for one another, friends are transformed precisely into that "life worth living." Where the Kantian approach asked, "How should I act?" or "What shall I do?" the virtue approach asks "How shall I live and how shall I become a person who lives in this way?"

The role of friendship in the modern ethical theory influenced by Kant is minimal, and even seen as an obstacle to the ethical life. The moral agent is not a person who has developed a moral character, but a person who is best able to act on abstract and universal principles of justice. The view of the moral self as purely rational implies that the emotional intimacy of particular friendship can provide no significant insight into one's moral self. In virtue ethics, on the other hand, the development of the moral character is accomplished precisely through friendships. Thus in the return to a consideration of virtue ethics, friendship becomes necessary for the development of virtues as states of soul or character. This has occasioned the return of interest in the understanding of friendship as constitutive of our very humanity. Descriptions of friendship from the ancients onward have received renewed attention. The longstanding and simplistic, Reformation objection to friendship—that *philia*-love is a lesser love than the ideal Christian *agapē*-love—no longer convinces. Rather, we read in recent Western literature that only in and through particular friendships of *philia* is *agapē*-love learned and achieved. Paul Wadell, a proponent of virtue ethics, puts it nicely:

---

15. Cf. J. L. Ackrill, "Aristotle on *Eudaimonia*," in *Essays on Aristotle's Ethics*, ed. Amelie Oksenberg Rorty (Berkeley: University of California Press, 1980) 24. For Aristotle's definition of *eudaimonia* as "final end," see his *Nicomachean Ethics* 1097b, 1–7.

when friends are brought together by a mutual love for God and a desire to follow Christ, their friendship is a relationship in which they learn the ways of God, imitate Christ, and thus learn to embrace those they hitherto ignored. In this context, *agapē* is not something other than friendship, but describes a friendship like God's, a love of such generous vision that it looks upon all men and women not as strangers but as friends.[16]

As a proponent of virtue ethics, Stanley Hauerwas has argued for many years that the Christian church must become the type of community in which the demands of mutuality present in the highest friendships are to be discovered and nourished.[17] In terms of the relation between *agapē* and *philia*, Hauerwas says

one might say that *philia* in the Christian church forms Christians to embody the love theologians have described as *agapē*. . . . it is not that that we Christians are formed by *philia* to become individuals who can individually practice *agapē*. Rather it is that we are formed by *philia* in the church to become a community which in its corporate life in the world loves the world in the manner of *agapē*, whose practice it has learned in seeking to conform itself to the God who is in Christ.[18]

In the communion of the Church we become friends with those who share a common vision of the Good, the Truthful, and the Beautiful. We do not grow in grace by acquiring "knowledge" about how we ought to live, but by the Spirit's prompting we develop friendships within the Church in which we seek the fullness of Christ for the other. Thus the Christian is called to rebuke his friends in the church community: ". . . if your brother sins against you, go to him and tell him his fault" (Matt 18:15). This text is immediately followed by Peter's query about how many times he should forgive his brother "not seven times, but seventy times seven" (18:22). Rebuke of friends in the community of the Church is

---

16. Paul Wadell, *Friendship and the Moral Life* (South Bend: University of Notre Dame Press, 1989) 96.

17. In this discussion, of course, we are speaking consistently of friendships based on goodness and virtue. This is the third of the types of friendship described by Aristotle. The first two types of friendship are first, of pleasure and, second, of usefulness. Aristotle says that "these two kinds are friendships only incidentally . . . ." (*Nicomachean Ethics* 1156a).

18. Stanley Hauerwas and Charles Pinches, *Christians Among the Virtues: Theological Conversations with Ancient and Modern Ethics* (South Bend: University of Notre Dame Press, 1997) 82.

always within the context of love and forgiveness, desiring the very best for the other in Christ. St. Augustine wrote to his old friend Marcianus, rejoicing that Marcianus has become a catechumen, "and thus fully a friend." "Although you seemed to love me greatly," says Augustine, "you were not yet my friend" (*Ep.* 258, 3).[19] Only when Marcianus became a catechumen did they have a united devotion to a shared vision of the good in which they would journey together and assist each other in the acquisition of virtues. Augustine points to the two great commandments of love of God and neighbor and writes to Marcianus, "If you with me will hold these two most firmly, our friendship will be true and everlasting and will unite us both with one another, and with the Lord himself" (*Ep.* 258, 3). In Aelred of Rievault's twelfth-century treatise *On Spiritual Friendship*, Aelred will intensify the previous teachings on friendship by suggesting that the tradition's reflection on Scripture leads to the formulation *Deus amicitia est* (God is friendship).

But something more needs to be said about the nature of the erotic that is present in friendship-love, especially in the light of our culture's appropriation of the teaching of Freud at the beginning of the twentieth century and his reduction of the erotic to the sexual.[20] I have suggested that the erotic was understood to be an element of friendship-love for the Ancient Greeks and Latins—Plato, Aristotle, Cicero, etc. At least as early as the third century, Origen's "fruitful alliance of Christian *agapē* and Platonic *eros*" ensured that the Christian mystical theology would embrace *eros* as accompanying both *agapē* and *philia*-love. Gregory of Nyssa says that *eros* is *agapē* "stretched out in longing." In his *Divine Names*, Dionysius in the first (or sixth) century sometimes suggests that *eros* is more divine than *agapē*, and in the end simply says that the sacred writers regard *eros* and *agapē* as having one and the same meaning. The erotic component of friendship-love is clearly manifested in the continuing interest in and interpretation of the Song of Songs until the very end of the Middle Ages.

But, to continue a theme, the place of the erotic in the divine activity of creation and redemption, in the soul's longing for God, and in

---

19. As cited by Robert D. Crouse in "Love and Friendship in Medieval Theology: Aristotle, St. Augustine, St. Thomas and Dante," in *Christian Friendship*, ed. Susan Harris (Charlottetown: St. Peter, 2005) 140–41.

20. In the following discussion I am especially indebted to Sarah Coakley, "Pleasure Principles: Toward a Contemporary Theology of Desire," *Harvard Divinity Bulletin* 33:2 (2005) 20–33.

human relationships generally, was largely devalued and put aside at the same time as friendship-love was devalued in the sixteenth century. Not surprisingly, in the mid-twentieth century erotic love suffered an even worse trashing by Anders Nygren than he had given to friendship-love. We can track the movement of Nygren's critique: *agapē* is the Christian love of Jesus in the New Testament—graced, God-given, sacrificial, downward-moving, unselfish. Nasty *eros*, "desire" or "longing," in contrast, is acquisitive, human-centered, upward moving, egocentric, and needy. For Nygren the erotic urge is frightening and alarming, entirely uncontrollable. Nygren's false characterization of both *philia* and *eros* has been shown by many. Sarah Coakley suggests that "it is Anders Nygren's famous study of *Agapē* and *Eros*, rather than the secular Freud, that has actually played a wider cultural role here than is normally recognized in undermining the efforts at a modern Christian theology of desire."[21] She rejects Nygren's misinterpretation of Freud that the erotic is to be understood only in terms of sexual attraction. Coakley locates in Freud's early writings the roots of the present sexualization of all forms of relationships in Western culture, but she also traces a development in his writings that shows that Freud later came to define *eros* in much more traditional terms as the drive that presses toward the future and new life. In his later writings Freud assents explicitly to Plato's theory of the erotic "ascent" to Beauty in the *Symposium*. She argues that Freud did not at all counsel that the repression or sublimation of libido (physical, biological, sex drive) was necessarily harmful. In fact Freud argues that very often such repression of libido simply is necessary.

In her analysis of Gregory of Nyssa's *De virginitate*, Coakley points out how Gregory recollects the positive role of *eros* in all human relationships. Gregory explains that all erotic desire, whether for the married or for the celibate, requires a proper channeling toward God through the disciplines of deep prayer and ascetic perseverance. A key point for Coakley is that these spiritual disciplines for the proper and salvific channeling of desire are required for all Christians, whether married or celibate. She concludes:

> Gregory's vision of desire as thwarted, chastened, transformed, renewed, and finally intensified in God, bringing forth spiritual fruits of *agapē* and *leitourgia* [service to others, especially to the poor] in a number of different contexts, represents a way beyond

21. Coakley, "Pleasure Principles," 20–33.

and through the false modern alternatives of repression and libertarianism, between *agapē* and *eros*, and has curiously more points of contact with the real Freud than the imaginary Freud of American popular consciousness.[22]

To summarize thus far, lately there has been a renewed interest in philosophical and theological literature about the nature and role of friendship in contemporary political life generally, about ethical thinking, and about the Christian life of holiness. I began this essay with a look at Florensky's letter on friendship that gathered in many of the classical and Christian themes in the tradition that have regained currency in the past several decades. Friendship-love is inclusive of *eros*, *philia* and *agapē*. It is the means by which we grow in virtue. For the Christian life it is the means by which we are made holy, by degrees. Thus we learn to live with a reality that we cannot mold to our own purpose. Through the activity of friendship-love within the community of the Church our lives are transformed and made capable of *agapē*-love of both friend and enemy. Christian friends look to their Lord who exemplifies the virtues consistent with divinity: both friends will seek, in common, to imitate their Lord and thus grow slowly into the character of God. But within his discussion of friendship, Florensky also drew attention to the notion of formal "covenanted friendships" within the Christian tradition. In 1914 he spoke of the "indissolubility" of friendship, as strict, he says, "as the indissolubility of marriage." Yet for Florensky these friendships, which would later be called "same-sex" unions, though erotic, are not sexual in nature at all. The exchange of the crosses during the rite symbolizes the mutual *ascesis* or life of renunciation within the friendship. In this renunciation Florensky locates the essential difference between friendship and marriage. He says,

> marriage is "two in one flesh," while friendship is two in one soul. Marriage is unity of flesh, *homosarchia*, while friendship is unity of souls, *homopsychia*.[23]

Now we turn directly to the question before the Anglican Church of Canada and ask how our consideration of friendship-love might contribute to the debate about the permissibility of same-sex marriages in the Christian church. A dominant theme in modern American culture,

---

22. Ibid., 20–33.
23. Florensky, *Pillar and Ground of the Truth*, 325.

expressed in many ways in Christian churches, is that this friendship love is given its highest expression in marriage. As the Hallmark wedding bulletin cover puts it: "Today I will marry my best friend." But is friendship (or the sanctification of friendship) the essence of marriage? Is marriage but another particular form of friendship?

Some of the leading Christian advocates for same-sex marriages describe marriage as a state of life in which gay or lesbian couples take life-long vows of monogamous fidelity so that they can grow in sanctification. Eugene Rogers argues in several articles that Christian theologians understand marriage only shallowly as the making licit of sexual satisfaction. Rather, Rogers insists, marriage is better understood as a state of life that provides opportunity for sanctification. Homosexual orientation is described as the inability of the gay or lesbian to experience the fullness of friendship-love in persons of the opposite sex. Gays and lesbians encounter the other (and thus discover themselves) in relation to persons of the same sex.[24] In fact, Rogers eloquently describes how the married couple provide for one another the friendship-love that I have described in this article, mirroring one another's souls and "exposing and healing each other's flaws over time." Rogers tries to clinch his argument for same-sex marriage saying, "No conservative has yet seriously argued that gay and lesbian couples need sanctification any less than heterosexual ones.... It is evil to attempt to deprive people of the means of their own sanctification." In the light of our presentation of friendship-love, I would say that Rogers presents a convincing argument that same-sex couples must not be deprived of the deep friendship that is required for their sanctification. His conclusion follows, however, for same-sex *marriage* only if marriage is understood solely as a specific type of friendship. There is no doubt that in the tradition of the Church friendship is an extremely important part of any Christian marriage. When children are involved, the parents must model, as much as they are given grace to do so, a friendship love that includes a fullness of *agapē* and a positive and healthy affirmation of the erotic, directing the erotic in such a way that the third person in every Christian relationship (God) is made present.

---

24. This particular claim is found in Eugene Rogers's unpublished article, "Marriage as a Discipline of Sanctification," 2005. Rogers cites David M. McCarthy, "The Relationship of Bodies: A Nuptial Hermeneutics of Same-Sex Unions," *Theology and Sexuality* 4 (1998) 73–95. Quotations in this paragraph are from Rogers, 2005.

Further, there is no doubt that wonderful and grace-filled friendships of man/man and woman/woman have been present in the Christian community throughout its history. It is not only a recent phenomenon for two Christian men or two Christian women to know the congruent grace of a romantic "falling in love" with one another and desiring to spend their lives together in joy and fidelity. But why is it only now that the Church is challenged doctrinally and pastorally to define these loving and grace-filled relationships as marriage?

The most common answer is that we now know more about the psychology of persons such that we have discovered that some men can only have the deepest emotional, physical, spiritual, and romantic intimacy with other men, and likewise that there are some woman who can only know the joy of sharing their souls profoundly and intimately with other women. But this discovery still begs the question: Why should the Church consider marriage to be the appropriate state of life for two Christian men or two Christian women who love each other deeply and commit themselves to lives of fidelity, intimacy, and sacrifice for each other? Ultimately, it is the Church's understanding of marriage that will determine whether marriage is the appropriate state of life for such grace-filled relationships. In what follows I suggest that the creeping sexualization of human relationships in the twentieth century that convinces us that we are sexual beings and that all relationships are ultimately sexual, has prompted the contemporary Church to begin to understand marriage in a way that deviates from the understanding of marriage as known in the tradition of the Church. The Church has come to see marriage as a state of life intended for the living out of a profound, intimate, and sexualized friendship. Intimacy has been confused with sexual expression such that the highest friendship is understood to require marriage because marriage is that state of life where the Church allows the type of sexual expression that nourishes and fulfills our deepest needs for intimacy and friendship love.

Recent changes to the Marriage Canon of the Anglican Church of Canada and the marriage liturgy of the *Book of Alternative Services* reflect this shift in understanding and push the Anglican Church of Canada decidedly in the direction of same-sex marriages. The Solemn Declaration of 1893, the founding document of the Anglican Church of Canada, locates its formal doctrinal understanding of Christian marriage in the 1662 *Book of Common Prayer*. Its description of marriage is coherent with that of the history and tradition of the Church. There we read that there are three purposes of marriage: (1) "It was ordained for the procreation of children to be brought up in the fear and nurture of the Lord . . . ."; (2) "It was ordained for a remedy against sin, and to avoid fornication . . . ."; and (3) "It was ordained for the mutual society, help and comfort that the one ought to have of the other in both prosperity and adversity." It should be noted that, in the second reason given for marriage, we still see the ancient Christian view that marriage is for those who not have "the gift of continency," (i.e., virginity and the single life). Canada introduced its own *Book of Common Prayer* in 1918, outlining the same purposes but removing the reference to the gift of continency, happily replacing the language of "remedy for sin, and to avoid fornication" with the much more positive language of the "hallowing of the union betwixt man and woman." In this articulation of the purpose of marriage, friendship, the hallowing of the spiritual, emotional, psychological bond, and procreation, were all somehow related.

It was *The Book of Alternative Services* of 1985 that introduced the significant shift in understanding of marriage. Marriage is now described as being for (1) "mutual comfort and help," (2) "that they may know each other with delight and tenderness in acts of love," and (3) procreation as optional. This liturgy thus institutionalizes the notion that the relationship between the couple—the friendship—is the primary purpose of marriage. The optional character of procreation cannot be interpreted as an attempt to be pastorally sensitive to those who cannot have children for physical reasons of age, infirmity, impotency, etc. Rather, many people today are simply choosing not to have children—in marriages not open, morally or physically, to the procreation of children. The role of sexual activity is tied to procreation only as an option, but its primary role is to enrich the relationship itself. This new understanding of the purpose of marriage is reflected in the 1967 version of the Marriage Canon, which gives as a purpose for marriage, "the creation of a relationship in which sexuality may serve personal fulfillment in a community of love." In other words, marriage is for the creation of a friendship in which sexual intimacy plays a significant part. Thus the deepening and lifelong expression of profound friendship becomes the sole purpose for marriage. It is thus little wonder, given this understanding, that when married couples feel that friendship is dissolving or not blossoming as they would like, they will think their marriage has come to an end. How else should they think? As Church, we have taught them to think in this way. In sincerity, in piety, with integrity, couples that do not develop or sustain friendship in their marriages will get out of one marriage, and try another, and perhaps even another, until they find the friend and friendship in Christ that they seek.

This development of the understanding of marriage through liturgical change and revision of the Marriage Canon in the Anglican Church of Canada is consistent with (and encouraged by) shifts of thinking evidenced by successive Lambeth Conferences during the first half of the twentieth century. The 1908 Lambeth Conference referred to the "reverent use of the married state" (Resolution 43), and the 1920 Conference referred to "the paramount importance in married life of deliberate and thoughtful self-control" (Resolution 68). Both of these comments are related to the Conference's rejection of birth control. At the Lambeth Conference in 1930, however, the Anglican Church made a fundamental departure from the Christian moral tradition in matters of sex and sexuality when it shifted from the thinking of the previous two Lambeth Conferences and declared that there is a role for artificial means of birth control in the sexual relationships of married persons. Whether the participants of Lambeth 1930 understood the significance of their determination, certainly Pope Pius XI recognized that Lambeth 1930 represented a major departure from the tradition of the Church. His encyclical *Casti Connubii* (*Chaste Marriage*) can be interpreted as a direct response to Lambeth 1930. The encyclical reads, in part:

> 54. *Since, therefore, the conjugal act is destined primarily by nature for the begetting of children, those who in exercising it deliberately frustrate its natural power and purpose sin against nature and commit a deed which is shameful and intrinsically vicious.*
>
> 56. *Since, therefore, openly departing from the uninterrupted Christian tradition some recently have judged it possible solemnly to declare another doctrine regarding this question, the Catholic Church, to whom God has entrusted the defense of the integrity and purity of morals, standing erect in the midst of the moral ruin which surrounds her, in order that she may preserve the chastity of the nuptial union from being defiled by this foul stain, raises her voice in token of her divine ambassadorship and through Our mouth proclaims anew: any use whatsoever of matrimony exercised in such a*

> way that the act is deliberately frustrated in its natural power to generate life is an offense against the law of God and of nature, and those who indulge in such are branded with the guilt of a grave sin.

What Pius XI pointed out here is that at Lambeth 1930, for the first time, a church claiming to stand within the Christian moral tradition had explicitly and officially said that sexual intercourse in itself, as an act unrelated to procreation, is one of the goods of marriage.[25]

Almost two decades ago, the present Archbishop of Canterbury boldly reflected upon the Anglican Church's approval of the use of contraception. His words are even more clearly truthful for a church that imposes no limits on the use of contraception—i.e., a church that marries people who intend to use contraception to prevent any children being born within the marriage, and for whom sexual intimacy is solely for building and maintaining relationship, never open to procreation:

> In a church that accepts the legitimacy of contraception, the absolute condemnation of same-sex relations of intimacy must rely either on an abstract fundamentalist deployment of a number of very ambiguous texts, or on a problematic and non-scriptural theory about natural complementarity, applied narrowly and crudely to physical differentiation without regard to psychological structures.[26]

In the light of the current widespread teaching that marriage is the highest friendship, and that the role of sexual activity within marriage is formative, expressive, and productive of that friendship (that the couple "may know each other with delight and tenderness in acts of love"), the argument of Eugene Rogers is sure. It is simply wrong to deprive same-sex couples of this highest form of friendship. Likewise, it is little wonder that thoughtful, pious, and sincere Anglicans should conclude that the type of covenanted same-sex friendships found in the Christian tradition (*adelphopoiesis*) is akin to same-sex marriage, either fully or pointing toward it. Our culture has sexualized intimacy such that marriage has become the form of which all other friendships are lesser imitations. To suppose that these covenanted life-long brotherhoods and sisterhoods

---

25. I am indebted to the Rev'd Eric MacDonald for this example, given in an unpublished paper presented to a local Anglican Clericus meeting in Nova Scotia in 2005.

26. Rowan D. Williams, "The Body's Grace," in *Theology and Sexuality*, ed. Eugene Rogers (Oxford: Blackwell, 2002) 309–21, at 320.

in the Christian tradition were a grace-filled type of profound friendship that demonstrated *philia, agapē,* and *eros* love but without sexual intimacy, is to see these relationships as just short of marriage. In our sexualized culture, these relationships are lacking something that could be provided if only they became full marriages.

CONCLUSION

In this paper I have tried to suggest that friendship is necessary to becoming fully human. Friendship, in its very many forms and manifestations, is the means by which we grow in Christian virtue and holiness. Our friendship with God in Christ transforms our character such that we become holy, and our friendships with one another are part of that activity of the formation of this virtuous life. It is in this context that the whole question of same-sex relationships must be understood. Christians should not be denied any of the forms of human friendship by which we come to know our holiness and communicate the character of God. Some forms of deepest friendships include the desire to live together in community, at least the church community.

The Scriptures, as understood within the unbroken tradition of the Church, speak of marriage as a state of life in which a male and female couple enters into a relationship that is at least morally open to the possibility of the procreation of children. The married relationship is outward looking in that it is also for the sake of others: for the potential for children to be born and raised within family. This relationship is permanent until the death of one or other of the married partners. It is a relationship that echoes the love that eternally binds together Christ and his Church. Thus, marriage is not simply friendship, even though it is a relationship in which there is every expectation that friendship-love, inclusive of *philia, agapē,* and *eros*, should flourish.

Finally, throughout the history of the Church, particular friendships that have developed between man/man and woman/woman have been recognized as such a means of God's grace that these friendships have been blessed, offered to God in prayer, and expressed in covenant form. Such friendships include living together in the light of God's presence and love, sharing in a life of sacrifice for the other, and seeing one's soul mirrored in the other by which such friends grow in holiness. These friendships (expressive of *philia, agapē,* and *eros*) reflect God's character, and his kingdom is made more real among us when we celebrate these friendships. If we either deny the reality of God's grace as expressed in this particular form of the highest of friendships, or if, equally, we deny these friendships by turning them into marriages, the kingdom will be less present among us.

And thus the title of this paper, "Friendship: The End of Marriage." That is, if friendship is the end (the sole purpose) of marriage, then friendship is the end (the destruction) of marriage.

4

Bodies without Borders

Desire, Abjection, and Human Sexuality in Recent Theology

Jane Barter Moulaison

PART ONE: *The Secular City*

I

I begin with a tale of two cities. The first is a marketplace where bodies are bought and sold, and the economy is built up through the persistent and unending exchange of sexual goods. There can be no limits placed upon consumption, and the city complies by offering up ubiquitous venues for personal expression and fulfillment. There is, in this city, no object that does not carry with it the promise of sexual fulfillment, and there is no subject too young or too old to become a producer or consumer of sexual goods. The citizens of this city believe themselves to be governed by their own individual choice—but their freedom consists chiefly in the capacity to choose among various commodities. These products include an endless parade of sexual possibilities and adventures. All of these will promise to fulfill our yearning, while all will offer only the kinds of goods that will, inevitably, both frustrate our longing and reproduce it. In spite of this city's discourse about cosmopolitan diversity, this city is a monolith, and globalization simply means the rapid extension of the sexual marketplace's reach. Fulfillment, expression, freedom—these are the signposts of the secular city, yet such signs point nowhere but to the endless cycle of simulation.

The Church is right to be alarmed about this city. It is right to call attention to the peculiar ways in which sexual desire has been shaped, not by its own confession, but by the libidinal economy of neo-liberal capitalism. Yet, there is nobody—gay nor straight, male nor female, Christian nor non-Christian—who has not traveled to, or inhabited, or been inhabited by, this city.[1]

II

Not so long ago, feminists used to decry the objectification of women through the machine of pornography, wanting to ban the sale of magazines like *Hustler* and *Playboy* because they, as the old slogan used to go, "tell lies about women." Given the sheer ubiquity of pornography, the fetishization of beauty, and the normalization of plastic surgery, the old slogan seems a trifle restrained: pornography does not tell lies about some stable reality called women—it creates women as it creates men, and thus it creates a kind of truth. And the truth it tells is that in the city—that is, the city that most of us inhabit daily and hardly notice—the simulacrum has become the ideal, and the real that remains—the particular, the unassimilated, the undesirable—has become the abject. I will return to this abject as a subject in a few moments as I tell the tale of another city.

PART TWO: *The Eternal City*

I

The nihilism of this secular city has, in recent years, been identified and decried by a movement[2] known as Radical Orthodoxy. Radical Orthodoxy represents a retrieval of classical theological sources in an ef-

---

1. Here, among the Radical Orthodox theologians, Graham Ward is particularly consistent in his fidelity to the Augustinian notion of the mixed nature (*permixtum*) of the City of Man [sic] and the City of God.

2. See James K. A. Smith on the aversion among those identified with Radical Orthodoxy to being labeled a "movement." James K. A. Smith, *Introducing Radical Orthodoxy: Mapping a Post-Secular Theology* (Grand Rapids: Baker, 2004) 63–67.

fort to critique and transform contemporary accounts of human agency and meaning. As one of its chief proponents, Graham Ward, writes,

> Radical orthodoxy looks at "sites" that we have invested much cultural capital in—the body, sexuality, relationships, desire, painting, music, the city, the natural, and reads them in terms of the grammar of the Christian faith; a grammar that might be summed up in the various creeds. In this way Radical Orthodoxy must view its own task as not only doing theology but being itself theological—participating in the redemption of Creation.[3]

For the purposes of this paper, I will examine just two intimately related sites within Radical Orthodoxy's purview: the city and the body,[4] while I will also limit my analysis to the writings of John Milbank on these. Milbank follows St. Augustine in writing of an alternative city, another body, which is governed not by the vicissitudes of worldly power and avarice, but by an unseen, but nevertheless real foundation. This foundation is peace and plentitude arising from God's gratuitous and unending love of the world.

It is here, in this celestial city, that citizens are shaped, not to exchange limited and manufactured goods, but to participate in a charity that enables radical generosity and reciprocity. This is because the gifts that citizens offer one another are themselves derived from the ineffable and inexhaustible depth that is God.

The economy of this other city, then, is one of plenitude rather than competition. And its dynamic is not consumption, a mere parody of desire, but rather right desire. Desire, arising from plenitude rather than lack, is also a desire arising from God rather than sin. Such desire is not fuelled by the competitive marketplace where bodies are exchanged. Instead, desire arises from the love of God toward humanity that calls us to return. This desire, right desire, is non-possessive even while it is passionately, and indeed erotically, engaged. Right desire can never be possessive or exploitative, for it is fundamentally participation in divine being, thus being formed and transformed by what we receive.

---

3. Graham Ward, "Radical Orthodoxy and/as Cultural Politics," in *Radical Orthodoxy?—A Catholic Enquiry*, ed. Laurence Paul Hemming (Aldershot: Ashgate, 2000) 103.

4. Although I must note that the body, in spite of its seeming self-evidence, is an enormously slippery concept. As Mary Douglas writes, "Just as it is true that everything symbolises the body, so it is equally true that the body symbolises everything else." Mary Douglas, *Purity and Danger: An Analysis of Concepts of Pollution and Taboo* (London: Routledge & Kegan Paul, 2002) 122.

The form of citizenship in this city is that of harmonious self-donation, which arises from recognition of the transitory nature of all our desires, and that refers these to that which is infinite. This does not entail a passing over or suppression of longing for the world or of bodily desires, but it means, rather, the *rectification* of desire. The rectification of desire involves mutual giving and receiving among the body's constituent parts. It is thus that Milbank affirms difference, seeing desire as working precisely through our attraction to one another as other as the means by which the self is turned outward. Thus the Church becomes the celestial city *in via* as it participates truly in the rule of charity in the redemptive order.

Desire in Milbank's celestial city arises from being arrested and enchanted by the non-assimilable difference that the other presents. Desire seeks not to absorb this otherness, but to delight in it, to engage it, and to respond to it. This distinctly Christian aesthetic can be compared to the musical movement of Baroque:

> Baroque hierarchy . . . is instead the appearance of the divine self-realization in finitude, and therefore as a vertical sequence up which each individual can contemplatively and actively rise. . . . God's love for what he creates implies that the creation is generated within a harmonious order intrinsic to God's own being.[5]

God's inner-triune being, according to Milbank, is pure *affinity* that flows abundantly toward humanity, toward that which is other, and therefore represents self-offering love. According to Milbank, human desire must be similarly turned outward toward the other in her difference:

> [A]s Augustine saw, the primacy (or equal primacy) of desire implies that "individuality" arises only through the constant rupturing and "externalization" of the subject. To contemplate is now to desire the other, to enter further into relation both with God and human beings and angels.[6]

Masculinity and femininity represent the paradigm of an inherent affinity that works through difference. Milbank views postmodernity as dominated by an erotics of narcissism that despises the mysterious difference of men and women, thus undercutting the possibility of a

---

5. John Milbank, "The Other City," in *Theology and Social Theory: Beyond Secular Reason*, 2nd ed. (Oxford: Blackwell, 2006) 436–37.

6. Ibid., 276.

true community. Sexual difference is not to be denied, neither is it to be considered of such a dissonance that exchanges between men and women can only be confrontational. Rather, desire works through, but never dissolves, sexual difference. Sexual difference, although "mysterious and sublimely ineffable," is also self-evident and real, and as such it is the paradigmatic form of non-violent, mutual participation in the celestial city:

> There can only be love, if there is ecstatic reciprocity and interplay of characters who *naturally belong together*.[7] [italics mine]

Thus Milbank rejects both the liberal feminist advocacy for the relativization of sexual difference, and neglects the postmodern feminist insistence on the profoundly disciplinary nature of our sexual performances.[8] In any event, Milbank opts for an alternative that has surprising resonance with the logic of radical feminism, which seeks not to question gender differences, but rather to *enhance* them. As Milbank writes:

> Rather the question of what is really desirable—an equality of the sexes without sexual difference (and an entirely inexpressible difference is no difference, even if one must struggle forever to articulate it), or a new equality of the sexes which seeks to enhance a sexual difference that it also affirms—teleologically and eschatologically.[9]

Milbank's swooning over the "new equality" of the sexes—one which seeks to enhance a sexual difference that it "also affirms" seems strikingly un-new. Milbank's eschatological yearning for a time when, to paraphrase the great theologian Archie Bunker, "girls were girls and men were men" is, in my judgment, a fairly predictable although tortuous, return to a gender essentialism—a framework that has never served women particularly well. Furthermore, he attacks the erosion of sexual difference as merely rooted within the logic of capitalist, postmodern nihilism. For, in his judgment, the uprooting of desire from "relatively constant essence" written in nature is a tactic of the marketplace that depends upon restless, nomadic experimentation. He enlists French

---

7. Ibid., 203.

8. It is, this second form of analysis, in my view, that will profoundly challenge the logic of the first city that I described—especially as it concerns the unrelenting sexual oppression of women.

9. Milbank, "Other City," 207.

literary critic Luce Irigaray to buttress his claim that it is precisely the *erosion* of sexual difference, and not its preservation, that is the source of misogyny.

Yet Irigaray's writings have long been interpreted in precisely the opposite ways from what Milbank suggests. According to her interpreters, Irigaray's location of the female body as a site for *l'écriture feminine* is not an essentialist move, but a heuristic and provisional one. It is an effort to claim a space within phallocentric language—the only language that is yet articulated—in order to subvert it.[10] In any case, one does not need to be an expert on French feminist theory to be able to challenge Milbank's reading of the signs of the times. Far from postmodern culture engendering an eradication of sexual difference, cosmetic industries and popular culture seem rather to hyperbolize it. Women and men are incessantly subjected to disciplinary evaluations of whether they can live up to the phantasms of manufactured gender polarity.

Milbank will wish, nevertheless, to defend gender difference as that which is rooted in the good created order, and while he acknowleges certain dangers in formulating too terse a typology of gender differences, he hazards the following generalization:

> Men are more nomadic, direct, abstractive and forceful, women are more settled, subtle, particularizing and beautiful.[11]

A feminist might wish to ask not merely how adequately Milbank describes reality, but to what degree his generalizations prescribe reality. Further, to what degree does he quite literally circumscribe the political and ecclesial possibilities of women? For his formulation inscribes women into a private, apolitical domain while reinsribing men in a political order that denotes mastery, domination, and control. Not a particularly salutary description of either male or female, in my judgment. But more on this later!

Although Milbank considers male–female relations paradigmatic and necessary for the proper ordering of the city, he does acknowledge homosexual desire as "part of the richness of God's creation," a richness that also seeks to transcend the natural order as it hints toward the "life

---

10. See, for example, Carolyn Burke, "Irigaray Through the Looking Glass," *Feminist Studies* 7 (1981) 303.

11. John Milbank, *Being Reconciled: Ontology and Pardon* (London: Routledge, 2003) 207.

of angels."[12] Milbank argues thus because he wishes to acknowledge the importance of gender as a recognizably natural given. Therefore, the persistence of those who defy his classifications of gender will have to be somehow explained. According to Milbank, homosexuals are angelic because they point beyond the economy of affinity to one of pure identity. But because of this, their unions cannot be considered paradigmatic, and therefore cannot be sanctified, for this would be to usurp the normative role of heterosexual marriage in representing the gospel of affinity. We will return in a moment to a critique of Milbank's essentialist notions of both gender and sexual orientation, but for now I would like to raise the question tentatively that I will explore more fully later: to elevate women to the status of the beautiful, and gays to the sphere of angels, would seem at first glance to make them more than human; in fact, as I shall later argue, it renders them less so.

II

Presiding over the eternal city is the eternal Christ, God incarnate, whose power "was disclosed as consisting in utter self-giving which is immediately returned, as resurrection, and therefore also gift-exchange."[13] It is Christ who reconciles "nations to nations, race to race, sex to sex, ruler to subordinate, person to person."[14] Christ's death and defeat might have signaled the death and defeat of the possibility of reconciliation were it not for his enabling the Church truly to take up his form of existence. The existence and form of Christ's Body, that is the Church, is itself a triumph over death. As Milbank writes,

> The main stress [of the New Testament] is that, on the basis of the rejected one, a new sort of community is to be built. But this is only possible because the rejected one is, bizarrely, also the most envied, unrepeatable one. If abandonment is the last word, then . . . there is no real hope. But Christ was never merely abandoned. He failed to resist human power and went freely to his death because he knew that a merely human counter-power is always futile and temporary. But he also went to his death, and therefore was innocent of suicide (and perhaps only innocent for this reason) in trust of his return, his resurrection. . . .

12. Ibid., 207.
13. John Milbank, "Christ the Exception," *New Blackfriars* 82 (2001) 551–52.
14. Milbank, *Being Reconciled*, 103.

> Nothing can be taken from the impassible God, and nothing can be added to his sum.[15]

This comment on Christ's nature is tremendously important for our purposes insofar as it speaks to the shape of Christian desire. Christ's desire, his passion, according to Milbank, is characterized by gratuitous self-donation and return. Christ pours out an endless surplus of love and power, even in his seeming defeat. This is because he is never finally emptied; he is never merely abandoned by God. This is to say that, for Milbank, the angel of death passed over the God-man even in his agony upon the cross. For, as the impassible one, death, defeat, and abjection, cannot be a reality, but only a temporary and provisional moment on its way to a greater victory:

> We also live in Christ because this typical abandoned man was nonetheless God, in whom we all participate and from whom we all have our life.[16]

It is here that I wish to pause to consider the chief lacuna of Milbank's eternal city, and it seems to me to be intimately related to the problematic that I previously identified in Milbank's description of intra-human desire. Milbank's eternal city, although beautiful, is nonetheless, like the secular city, curiously reticent on the significance of the abandoned, the unbeautiful, the despised, and the abject. His Christology is brief in acknowledging the abjection of Christ on the cross, as it insists rather docetically that he was never finally abandoned, and never more than fully confident that his cause would be vindicated. His bodily suffering is undertaken primarily as a gesture of his freedom from and sovereignty over despotic coercion.

One might ask Milbank here the question that Gregory of Nazianzus posed to the Apollinarians, the Docetists of the fourth century: *Can Christ heal what he has not fully assumed*? Is the cross merely a way station on the road to reconciliation, or is it its *sine qua non*? One would do well to remember Karl Barth's words here:

> [W]e must not escape from this life. We must not take flight to a better land, or to some height or other unknown, nor to any spiritual Cloud-Cuckookland nor to a Christian fairyland. God has come into our life in its utter unloveliness and frightful-

---

15. Ibid.
16. John Milbank, "Atonement: Christ the Exception," in *Being Reconciled*, 103.

ness. That the Word became flesh also means that it became temporal, historical. It assumed the form which belongs to the human creature, in which there are such folk as this very Pontius Pilate—the people we belong to and who are also ourselves at any time on a slightly larger scale. It is not necessary to close our eyes to this, for God has not closed His either; He has entered into it all. . . .[17]

PART THREE: *Cities' Borders*

I

Thinking about sexuality and the body politic must be rooted firmly in this world, and must not seek to hide from its unloveliness. It is therefore the responsibility of the Church to consider not just those bodies that have conformed to a harmonious ordering—not those bodies that participate in the ineffable mystery of desire, but the abject, those whom philosopher Julia Kristeva calls, "the strayed subject [who] is huddled outside the paths of desire."[18] I wish therefore not to ponder the mystery of our sanctioned covenants, but rather to attend to those who wander on their borders—many of whose sexual lives tell stories other than the ones that the Church has, by and large, been willing to acknowledge. This includes the stories of hosts of refugees from our cities—gays and lesbians, and those whose gendered performances, by choice or necessity, exist at an angle to our prescribed gender roles.

Agamben and the Biopolitical

In order to consider the dynamic of sexual abjection I need to trace an important ideological slippage in recent Christian thought that is actually foreign to its thinking about bodies. I will draw on the writings of Italian philosopher Giorgio Agamben, whose notion of *biopolitics*, taken from Foucault and Arendt but modified considerably, helpfully identifies the fissure in classical Greek thought that severs bare life (*zoē*), the life aimed merely at the sustenance of bodies, from *bios*, the life of politics, the life protected and governed by a sovereign power. *Bios*, as opposed

---

17. Karl Barth, *Dogmatics in Outline*, trans. G. T. Thompson (New York: Harper, 1959) 109.

18. Julia Kristeva, *The Powers of Horror* (New York: Columbia University Press, 1982) 11.

to *zoē*, represents political rather than natural belonging. It is a belonging to a people based upon citizenry rather than birth. This separation is also apparent in the Greek demarcation of *oikos* and *polis*, private and public. For the Greeks, life outside the *polis* could only be godly or animal-like, but as such it offered a level of autonomy from sovereign power, as the *oikos* could be regulated from within (albeit through the sovereign-like power of the Father). The boundaries of sovereign authority are illuminated through the state of exception. Sovereign power is that which determines what is the exception, that is, who is on the outside of the law.[19] Modern biopolitics confuses the exception, that which is outside of the sphere of sovereignty, with the rule, thus bringing more and more of *zoē*—naked life—under sovereign surveillance and control. This depoliticizing of the subject legitimates increased sanctioning, control, and disenfranchising as a means of preserving the body politic. As Agamben writes, "Western politics, bare life, has the peculiar privilege of being that whose exclusions found the city of men."[20] For Agamben, the paradigmatic example of biopolitical power and dispossession is the concentration camp, where human beings are stripped of belonging except through apolitical and quasi-biological categories such as race, blood, mental retardation, homosexuality, and so on. Yet contemporary society is replete with these biopolitical ascriptions. As Agamben enumerates, "the voter, the worker, the student, but also the HIV-positive, the transvestite, the porno star, the elderly, the parent, the woman . . . all rest on naked life."[21]

The question, I am sure, that is on everybody's mind here is: What does this have to do with our theme of the Church and human sexuality? Insofar as our ecclesiologies are underwritten by a version of the modern state, we are in danger of reducing human beings in their irreducible singularity to bare life, even as we consider the members of the Church's body. For, all too often, in our debates about sexuality we decontextual-

---

19. See Giorgio Agamben, *Homo Sacer: Sovereign Power and Bare Life* (Stanford: Stanford University Press, 1998).

20. Agamben, *Homo Sacer*, 7. Agamben draws heavily on Walter Benjamin here. "The tradition of the oppressed teaches us that the 'state of emergency' in which we live is not the exception but the rule. We must attain to a concept of history that is in keeping with this insight." Walter Benjamin, "Theses on the Philosophy of History," in *Illuminations*, trans. Harry Zohn (New York: Schocken, 1989) 257.

21. Giorgio Agamben, *Means Without End: Notes on Politics*, trans. Vincenzo Binetti and Cesare Casarino (Minneapolis: University of Minnesota Press, 2000) 7.

ize human sexuality from relationships and communities, thus treating sex as discrete acts, and persons as biopolitical identities. This is particularly the case as we consider the "question" of the homosexual and the woman.

II

"Women are more settled, subtle, particularizing and beautiful" [italics mine], writes John Milbank.[22] The problem is not that feminists object to being described as subtle or beautiful, but that characterization is an inherently apolitical ascription that relegates women to a fundamentally private life. This description, purportedly founded within nature, is a reinstating of a particular form of political identity that not only excludes women from the public sphere, but locates them exclusively with the realm of bare life, which, according to the analysis I am suggesting, has become a domain of state surveillance. The ascription of the biopolitical category of woman is the first step toward her disenfranchisement, and, within the modern state at least, the exercise of discipline over her body.

Milbank's elevation of the homosexual to the sphere of angels is likewise to treat him as the abject—the more than human is still the unhuman, outside the boundaries of political existence, like women, children, slaves, and the gods in the Greek polis. Thus the category woman or homosexual is severed from the contours of a life narrative. It is thus that womanhood and homosexuality become the chief markers of identity within a body politic so that they might come to occupy a sphere of otherness. But human life can never be prescribed by a "specific biological vocation, nor is it assigned by whatever necessity; instead, no matter how customarily repeated, and socially compulsory, it always retains the character of possibility. . . ."[23]

Agamben's description of the singularity of the person, her unrepeatable and irreducible newness that exceeds every ascription of identity, has profound resonances with Christian anthropology. But this means reading Scripture in a way that is divested from reified or idealized accounts of what it means to be male or female, Jew or Greek, slave or free (Gal 3:28). It means, indeed, reading the Body apocalyptically.

---

22. Milbank, *Being Reconciled*, 207.
23. Agamben, *Means Without End*, 7.

76 *Desire, Vocation, and Friendship*

The Church as Messianic Community

Paul's great description in 1 Corinthians 12 of the body with many members would seem, at first glance, to be reinforcing Milbank's theme of harmonious ordering, were it not for verses 23 and 24:

> And those members of the body that we think less honorable we clothe with greater honor, and our less respected members are treated with greater respect; whereas our more respected members do not *need* this. But God has so arranged the body, given the greater honor to the inferior member. (1 Cor 12:23–24) [italics mine]

Paul subverts the common ancient trope of the community as body when he deems the "inferior member" (and here we are not wrong to read this also as a sexual metaphor) as needing the greatest honor. This is a subversion of social hierarchy, even as it is a recognition of the non-rational, "other" members of the body. At the head of this body, and always determined by him, is *Iēsous Christos*, Jesus the Messiah, who inaugurates not a new *form* of community, but a prophetic challenge to congealed and stable forms of religiosity. This moment is a coming together or constellation of history, a recapitulation in which time is shot through and through with possibility.[24]

In this fulfilled time, the Messiah calls persons from their vocations to a revocation, a hollowing out of any identity that might be considered natural or fundamental in a hierarchical ordering. This messianic calling makes all things new, including our relations to one another, which is no longer based upon anything else than being *called* to be a follower of the abjected Messiah.[25]

Such a vocation is an interruption and a hollowing out of any identity that is based upon previous notions of political or natural identity. Our status, our ethnicity, even our gender therefore are not to be confused with the finalities of ourselves. For the re-contextualization of all

---

24. The messianic kingdom is "not the goal of history but the end." Walter Benjamin, "Theses on the Philosophy of History," 312.

25. See P. Travis Kroeker, "Whither Messianic Ethics? Paul as Postmodern Political Theorist," *Journal of the Society of Christian Ethics* 25:2 (2005) 37–58, at 51: "Paul refers to himself frequently as *doulos*, slave of the Messiah. Paul now confounds this juridical term from within because the sovereign Lord whom the *doulos* serves is a crucified Messiah. As such, the condition of doulos is itself transformed; it stands for a general transformation of worldly-political-social conditions blasted out of the continuum of history."

our lives in the apocalyptic coming of the Messiah means an uprooting of our identities as fixed or necessary. This does not mean a revolutionary re-ordering of societies (which is likely merely to reverse rather than subvert hierarchical orderings), but it is a freeing to *use* our identities in ways that in suffering provide service to Christ and neighbor. Therefore, in the apocalyptic present coming of the Messiah, disciples are to "remain in the condition in which you were called" (1 Cor 7:20), and "make use of your present condition" (v. 21). This has enormous implications for gender, for members of the messianic community are now freed from the dictates of gender hierarchy because of the coming of Christ in whom the form of the old world is passing away. This does not mean that the gendered patterns of the passing world can be escaped, but they now are now to be *used* insofar as they are directed toward discipleship. As P. Travis Kroeker puts it:

> This nullification of worldly vocation is not abandoning it for an "elsewhere" but dwelling within it as in exile, in dispossession. This dispossession allows the power of God to transform it in keeping with its true condition or "figure," its "passing away" toward an "end" that lies beyond it. This transforming power is a kind of messianic "use" of the world that stands in opposition to "dominion" and possessiveness.[26]

Instead of an idealized account of the ordering of another city, Agamben writes of the messianic interruption in history as an unprecedented newness that is brought to all things. Here the angularity of the moment and of the singular is retained.[27] Agamben's apocalyptic reading of the coming community seeks to hold up the incommensurate, the dissonant, the abject—and all those cast out of the city. The Messiah who delivers Israel delivers not merely those who are inside its borders, but interrupts patterns of natural and political order as he calls those who are cast away, and attends particularly to those whose desires, aspirations, and hopes have been crushed under the weight of political expediency.[28]

---

26. Kroeker, "Whither Messianic Ethics?" 48.

27. Giorgio Agamben writes of the nativity crib as the great symbol of this newness: "the crib counterpoises the minutiae of history in what might call its nascent state, in which everything is mere separate shred and splinter, but each sliver is immediately and historically complete." *Infancy and History: On the Destruction of Experience.* (London: Verso, 2006) 144.

28. In this sense, Slavoj Žižek offers an important comment on Agamben and Benjamin's "angel of history": "we are dealing not with idealist or spiritualist teleology, but with the dialectical notion of a historical epoch whose 'concrete' definition has to

The two cities that I have described are rooted in desire—the first in a desire based upon lack; the second a desire based on affinity. The borderlands of the city call both types of desire into question. The abject interrupts the normal trajectories of desire offering instead a desire that is turned toward the negated, the forgotten, and the scorned. Agamben points to an otherworldly kind of desire—one that does not depend on affinity, but rather is directed ever toward the forgotten and the disruptive:

> In every instant, the measure of forgetting and ruin, the ontological squandering that we bear within ourselves far exceeds the piety of our memories and consciences. But the shapeless chaos of the forgotten is neither inert nor ineffective. To the contrary it is at work within us with a force equal to that of the mass of conscious memories, but in a different way. Forgetting has a force and a way of operating that cannot be measured in the same terms as those of conscious memory, nor can it be accumulated like knowledge. Its persistence determines the status of all knowledge and understanding. The exigency of the lost does not entail being remembered and commemorated; rather, it entails remaining in us and with us as forgotten, and in this way and only in this way, remaining unforgettable.[29]

Within a new community, based solely upon the apocalyptic coming of the Messiah, the abjected ones (including us all in our exigency and decomposition) are called from our forgottenness and are remembered. If the coming of the Messiah transfigures potentially all things, including and perhaps especially those things deemed abject or that are forgotten, then the new community is to be precisely the community that learns the skill to desire not the desirable, but rather the undesirable and the forgotten.[30]

---

include its crushed potentials, which were inherently negated by its reality." It is the "crushed" and the "negated" that the messianic light preserves and redeems. Slavoj Žižek, *The Fragile Absolute: Or, Why Is the Christian Legacy Worth Fighting For?* (London: Verso, 2001) 90.

29. Giorgio Agamben, *The Time That Remains: A Commentary on the Letter to the Romans*, trans. Patricia Dailey (Stanford: Stanford University Press, 2005) 40.

30. Agamben writes of the political nature of this remembering: "The alternatives at this juncture are therefore not to forget or remember, to be unaware or become conscious, but rather, the determining factor is the capacity to remain faithful to that which having perpetually been forgotten, must remain unforgettable. It demands [*esige*] to remain with us and be possible for us in some manner. To respond to this exigency is the only historical responsibility I feel capable of assuming fully." *Time that Remains*, 40.

III

The Church considered itself to be both an *oikos* and a *polis* even while it radicalized both types of social configurations (Eph 2:19). Christ thus abolished the ancient biopolitical order in calling into existence a new community that did not relegate bare life to a kind of exceptional status. Christ's sovereignty extended not merely to the *polis* but also to the *oikos*, and the form of his sovereignty was suffering service. If there is a polity that proceeds from this, it is that it becomes the task of the disciples of Christ to be a community whose desire is turned to the wanderers and the forsaken because we belong to a Messiah who was himself a forsaken sojourner. The people who have become skilled in this desiring are called the saints,[31] and they are themselves wanderers and the unassimilated in the cities' economies of desire. They are eunuchs (Matt 19:12), virgins,[32] widows, and ascetics of various sorts whose communion with the abjected members of the body serves as a reminder to the Church that its body politic[33] is never glory, but always weakness. For the Church has become the "rubbish heap of the world, the dregs of all things." (1 Cor 4:13).

---

31. See, for example, Stanley Hauerwas's fine essay, "To Love God, the Poor, and Learning," in Stanley Hauerwas and Romans Coles, *Christianity, Democracy and the Radical Ordinary: Conversations between a Radical Democrat and a Christian* (Eugene, OR: Cascade, 2008) 242, which speaks of Gregory of Nazianzus's sermons on leprosy. "[Gregory] was able to love the poor because, schooled by Christ, he had no reason to deny them or wish that they did not exist. His descriptions of those who suffered from leprosy were loving because he had learned to love Christ, and therefore could not help but love the afflicted, even those afflicted with leprosy."

32. Gregory of Nyssa speaks of virgins as occupying a "frontier" (*methorios*) between life and death. "But those who by virginity have desisted from this process have drawn within themselves the boundary line of death, and by their own deed have checked his advance; they have made themselves, in fact, a frontier between life and death, and a barrier too, which thwarts him." Gregory of Nyssa, *On Virginity*. Online: http://www.ccel.org/ccel/schaff/npnf205.ix.ii.ii.xiv.html.

33. See, for example, "It's worth wondering why so little of the agitation about sexual morality and the status of homosexual men and women in the Church in recent years has come from members of our religious orders; I strongly suspect that a lot of celibates do indeed have a keener sensitivity about these matters than some of their married fellow Christians. And anyone who knows the complexities of the true celibate vocation would be the last to have any sympathy with the extraordinary idea that sexual orientation is an automatic pointer to the celibate life; almost as if celibacy before God is less costly, even less risky, for the homosexual than the heterosexual." Rowan Williams, "The Body's Grace," in *Theology and Sexuality: Classic and Contemporary Readings*, ed. Eugene Rogers (Malden: Blackwell, 2002) 313.

The challenge that is before Christians is to so think about our body politic in ways that are not merely inclusive (for inclusivity can all too easily fall into the market's logic), but that refuse to be based on a condition of belonging or a fixed identity other than having been called by God. This means that however we carry on conversations about sexuality, gender, men, and women, we cannot conform to the kind of disciplinary language that seeks to categorize persons based merely on a kind of naked identity. For once we do this, we reduce life to a mere function, and the contours of a life-narrative to categories that render our brothers and sisters exceptional and abject. The safeguard against this lapse into abjectification is Christian friendship.

Becoming Friends

In two important essays, Stanley Hauerwas points a way forward for us in our inarticulacy around the meaning and nature of sexual identity. These are two essays on friendship: the first is titled "Gay Friendship: A Thought Experiment," and the second, an essay co-written with Charles Pinches, is titled "Friendship and Fragility." According to Hauerwas, friendship is not primarily an experience, but an activity,

> through which we acquire the skills necessary if we are to become people of practical wisdom. . . . We literally cannot do good without our friends, not simply because we need friends to do good, but because the self-knowledge necessary to do good comes from seeing ourselves through our friendships.[34]

Although Hauerwas draws liberally on Aristotle's notion of friendship's necessity for cultivating political subjects, he also radicalizes him in these two essays, which consider, respectively, the possibility of friendship with homosexuals, and between men and women. The latter type of friendship was, of course, a scandal to Greco-Roman society, and it prompted copious rumors against the early Christians for supposedly wild sexual indiscretion, which the early apologists had to refute. In a parallel apologetic, Hauerwas challenges Martha Nussbaum's interrogation of male–female friendship, which Nussbaum argues is inherently fragile, and vulnerable to the tragedy of infidelity, betrayal, and revenge. Against this, Hauerwas argues that our friendships as Christians can

---

34. Stanley Hauerwas, "Gay Friendship: A Thought Experiment," in Eugene Rogers, ed., *Theology and Sexuality*, 291.

never be finally tragic, because Christ has overcome tragedy reconciling the world to God and offering forgiveness and restoration. The implications of friendship for the problems that I have outlined in this paper in conversation surrounding gender and sexual identity are several.

Christian friendship is the undoing of the endless symbiosis of desire and abjection. It is an overturning of biopolitical categories because, when we become friends, such categories cannot be sustained. Further, friendship teaches us that categories such as gender and sexual orientation can never be exhaustive. The living flesh of a friend resists any ideal that may be supposed to exist *behind* terms such as man and woman, gay and straight. Gender or sexual orientation thus becomes only provisional markers that are properly contextualized within the community and a story. Identity is not a fixed or static given, but is at once a vocation to which we are called by God and a complex set of durable practices in a community that will disrupt, mold, and give them their proper orientation. Although friendship does not exhaust the meaning of Christian marriage, it is nevertheless a central activity within it as men and women receive the self-knowledge to grow into maturity through the quotidian and sustained practices of raising children, breaking bread, resting, and growing old together. It is within such friendships that the idea of woman, for example, can never dissolve into an abstraction, but rather is grasped as an irreducible singularity. To attempt to narrate such a singularity is always a partial task, even for those who are married, for there is always something that remains hidden, always a surprise, always a possibility.[35]

To be a friend to gays and lesbians and to seek an unidealized account of male–female friendship in our church is to be engaged in a re-narration of desire. It is such a re-narration that permits Christian marriage to escape the dictates of yet another impossible ideal, while it also permits the witness of those abjected from the economies of our desire—particularly women and those who are called homosexuals—a reprieve from the endless and oppressive hold of our accounts that abjectify. Friendship in Christ is also the character of the kind of community

---

35. See Agamben, *Means Without End*, 91, on the mystery of the human face: "The face is at once the irreparable being-exposed of humans and the very opening in which they hide and stay hidden. The face is the only location of community, the only possible city. And that is because that which in single individuals opens up to the political is the tragicomedy of truth, in which they always already fall and out of which they have to find a way."

that perceives the hope, that after our endless debates over these vexing issues, and though we find ourselves in a Church where we often experience neither intrinsic affinity nor desire, we nevertheless can anticipate reconciliation, because Christ has called us from the crossroads of our cities to his abundant banquet (Prov 8–9).

THE NUPTIAL MYSTERY
THE SACRAMENT OF MARRIAGE

5

The Nuptial Mystery

The Historical Flesh of Procreation

Ephraim Radner

I am here to talk about something called "the nuptial mystery." Linguistically, the phrase has its scriptural center in Eph 5:31–32. Citing Gen 2:24, Paul writes, "For this reason a man shall leave his father and mother and be joined to his wife, and the two shall become one flesh"; then he asserts: "this mystery is a profound one and I am saying that it refers to Christ and the church." Now, although the scriptural center of this phrase, nuptial "mystery," is found in these verses, there is far more in the Scriptures that pertains to it. After all, Paul calls it, literally, a "mega mystery"—*mega mysterion*—and this profundity and depth takes in, potentially, quite a bit. Indeed, the notion of a "nuptial mystery" has garnered a good bit of theological interest recently, both from traditionally oriented Roman Catholics especially, and from revisionist advocates of, for instance, gay marriage.

I will be touching on aspects of all this in my following remarks. But I want to signal up front what my central claim will be. For I want to insist that the "mystery" in the "nuptial mystery" of which Paul and the Bible and ultimately the Christian Church herself speaks, is, at its heart, *procreative*—generative in a child-producing way. I know that this will sound to many as reactionary in an unimaginative kind of way—as if what is at stake in understanding the nuptial mystery is indeed a more fertile and wide-ranging imagination than old conservatives like me can muster; and it will also appear to some as scripturally counter-intuitive, especially in light of something like Eph 5:32, which mentions nary a child in it.[1] Finally, to place procreation at the center of the nuptial mystery must appear to some as unrealistic—even cruelly so. Has not vowed celibacy always been seen as partaking of the nuptial mystery? And what of infertile married couples? Today, of course, contraception and artificial fertilization mechanisms have decoupled, literally, procreation from marriage altogether in some cases. "Face the facts!" they might say to me. Even conservatives committed to maintaining the marriage norm of heterosexual partnerships have followed Aquinas and Barth in decentering procreation from the nuptial essence, for just these reasons.

I will say a good bit more about these likely intuitions. But let me simply note here, in reverse reference to these worries: first, celibacy and infertility have always been addressed by the Christian tradition, not avoided; but the tradition has addressed them from *within* the symbolic system of procreative heterosexual marriage, for the latter gives semantic luminescence to the former, not the other way around, and so it should remain. Second, to the claim that even Ephesians says nothing about children: the claim is *prima facie* a false one, since what immediately follows Paul's discussion of husbands and wives are four verses that deal *precisely* with the relationship of children to parents: "Children, obey your parents in the Lord, for this is right" (Eph 6:1). The worry that procreation is a cultural importation to, especially, New Testament texts about marriage is based on a resolute desire to rule out scriptural context—both proximately (as in this case) as well as more broadly, as in the opening of the Gospels, or indeed as in the entire Old Testament (which itself ends, in Malachi, on the note with which Matthew begins—parents and children). Any purported scriptural argument that marginalizes procreation within the nuptial mystery has about it, I would argue, something of a Marcionite tinge. Perhaps it even has, as Christopher Roberts has recently argued, a Manichaean tinge as well: cut off the Old Testament,

---

1. See Rowan Williams, "The Body's Grace," in *Our Selves, Our Souls and Bodies: Sexuality and the Household of God*, ed. Charles Hefling (Boston: Cowley, 1996) and Eugene Rogers, *Sexuality and the Christian Body: Their Way into the Triune God* (Oxford: Blackwell, 1999) 204–13, 242–48; Williams showed his interest already in John Boswell's arguments in favor of relational over procreative character of marriage (as in the latter's *Rediscovering Gay History: Archetypes of Gay Love in Christian History* [London: Gay Christian Movement, 1982]).

and you have cut off the informing and sanctifying force of creation as a *good*.² Finally, as for the intuition that placing procreation at the center of the nuptial mystery is dully reactionary, let me say something briefly as to how imaginations might well be formed on this matter, indeed how they must necessarily be formed: that is, from *within* families and from within the procreative network of generations and peoples. It is *who we are*, each one of us, by definition. Where else, and indeed *why* else would the topic ever even come up? One may well choose to rule out these realities as theologically essential elements in discussing marriage, but in doing so there is at work, I think, a kind of natural analogy to scriptural Marcionitism—a simple and steadfast denial of history, that will not answer the question, "where now *did* you come from?"

I might answer it this way. My father's side of the family, for instance, is Jewish. And we know that Judaism has always placed a high value on having children and on extending the life of Israel's people through the dutiful act of childbearing. Certainly, in the context of my father's immigrant Jewish culture, driven by persecution and made supremely critical (in the eyes of many Jews anyway) by the European extermination of lived genealogy during the 1930s and 1940s, there were always hovering about and under our family life the pressures for child-conceiving and child-rearing. When articulated openly in this context (which, in my personal experience was rarely), the drive from broken memories into an embodied future—we shall and must survive those who would have us disappear!—was made explicit. Having within my family on this side, as we do, a few who would also say, Job-like perhaps, by contrast, "I will not bring children into this world"—read "a world that kills Jewish children"—stood, not so much as a rebuke to these larger family drives for memory through propagation, but as a ground motif of mortality upon and within which the drive was—and is!—necessarily enacted over time. Procreation for my Jewish family is troubled; but what isn't in this life? And the trouble is magnified and real precisely because it cannot be avoided.

My mother's side of the family, on the other hand, is Gentile to the core. Her's were the Poles who, through their own genealogies, drove my father's family across the oceans, and whose family stomped into the dust those Jews who remained, letting dust then join the air. Do Jews

---

2. Christopher Chenault Roberts, *Creation and Covenant: The Significance of Sexual Difference in the Moral Theology of Marriage* (New York: T. & T. Clark, 2007) 204–8, 225.

and Gentiles procreate differently and for different reasons? Maybe. Certainly, the needs are expressed differently. In the generation before my own, these expressions, of course, included the happy designations "kike" and "polak" as the bearers of the future. I only recently returned from the funeral of my aunt, my mother's sister, the one person who kept me bound still to this Gentile genealogy. I saw cousins there I had not seen in almost twenty-five years. The ties among us are long loosened, for a host of reasons. The shape of common life among this side of my family—several generations now of multiple divorces, and of single persons and gay persons—now marked the gathering in the pews at my aunt's funeral as one that had been washed up for decades against the reefs of modernity, not without bearing at the same time a grown in beauty and grace. The generations have indeed been breaking up on this side of the family, even as the struggle on the other side has, as it were, often been too heavy a burden to bear.

One needs to think about these contrasts—Jews pressing for children and memory and getting angry about it, Gentiles pressing back and disintegrating, "kikes" and "polaks" in their own interrelations—and what they mark and question. My own (Polish) mother committed suicide when I was a teenager. It is indeed difficult not to take this fact as an immovable questioning of the entire procreative press of generation. Although I have come to be able to accept the intolerability of anguish that my mother must have felt in her last years of troubled mind and heart, of mental illness I suppose, I still cannot help feel a squirm of dissonance whenever I hear the words in Hosea, which mention my own name, "How can I give you up, O Ephraim?" (11:8). I do not know how, I say to myself, but I know it is possible. Yet I hear these words from *God* that follow—"My heart recoils within me and my compassion grows warm and tender." And since they are from God, I realize this distant procreative love in human form must yet go further to reach its fulfillment. My imagination, that is, well realizes that what a human being recognizes as the place of child-bearing and child-raising, is all-too-ill-founded—not because it has been idolized, as some critics of procreative marriage have recently argued, but because its center in God's purpose has been obscured. God presses for life, for life to continue. It is *we* who resist it. Let us be clear on this simple dynamic.

And the passage from the Jews to the Gentiles is, historically, hardly one toward freedom from generative slavery, as if ethnic perpetuation is something the eschatologically liberated New Testament and the celibate Paul finally figured out how to do without—this, at least, is what some Christians who have proposed alternatives to procreative, and even non-heterosexual marriage, have argued. No, the passage from Jew to Gentile is one whereby the genealogy of God's love has been permitted, enabled, and empowered to keep us alive through time together. The gift of faith in a redeeming God is generational to Jew and Gentile alike. But I shall return to this later.

I want to end this somewhat meditative introduction simply by repeating my core claim: the center of the nuptial mystery is procreative. And for all the difficulties this claim entails, it remains unavoidable: we are not talking *first* of desire, or of self-worth in opening up to another, or of being caught up into the triune God—all alternative claims I will argue against—we are talking about *children*. We are talking about their possibility, their fragility and mortality, their challenge and gifts, their potential and real futures, their withholding and disappearance for another's coming. For William Whateley, whose early-seventeenth-century *Directions for Married Persons* was called by John Wesley the best work on marriage "in any either Ancient or modern tongue," the love that arises within and upholds the marriage of a man and a woman springs first, not from desire or attraction, but from a singular *purpose*. And the purpose is this: that together husband and wife might leave their first "family"—we note that in Paul's and Jesus's use of the Genesis verse, a man must "leave his father and mother"—to become the "roots of a new family," through whose children and household God's vineyard might have provided for it "new plants."[3] It is this "leaving," joining, and beginning that marks the historical force of genealogy. But of marriage thereby.

---

3. William Whateley, *Directions for Married Persons: Describing the Duties Common to Both, and Peculiar to Each of Them*, originally published as *A bride-bush, or wedding sermon* (1617) but reprinted by John Wesley in his Christian Library, vol. 24, (London, 1753) chapter 7. If the proportion of discussion is a marker of the author's intrinsic interests, Whateley is far more concerned with the relationship of the spouses, including simply and rather surprisingly the acts of intercourse, than he is on the place of children in this relationship. And, in this way he is representative of a growing Puritan emphasis. But counting pages here would also be theologically misleading with respect to Whateley's final sense of marriage's meaning, which places relational virtues at the service of something much larger that must essentially be ordered towards procreation, whatever its actual numerical results: the family. Witte, versus some scholars, is doubtful that marital love ever really supplants the priority of procreation in seventeenth-century reflection on marriage (see John Witte Jr., *From Sacrament to Contract: Marriage, Religion, and Law in the Western Tradition* (Louisville: Westminster John Knox, 1997) 262 n. 152.

But so far I am speaking only in assertions. Why would one argue for procreation as lying at the center of the nuptial mystery? In large part, after all, the wording of Paul has led interpreters in another direction: "I am saying that [this mystery] refers to Christ and the Church" (Eph 5:32 RSV). That is, as some read Paul, the leaving of one family and the making of another, in Whately's terms, is seemingly "about" something other than the families in question. And in light of this, many have assumed that human marriage is "really" about something else altogether *other* than the "human" element that marriedness only apparently assumes. So first let us ask this question: is marriage about that thing which is before our eyes, or is it about something else that is somehow "behind" what we see and touch? Is it about this or that particular *body*—the man and the woman—or about bodies "in general" or even "spirits" in general? Is it about bodies at all, or is it really about something greater than bodies, to which they point, or in which they participate? Is what is "mysterious" about the nuptial mystery the fact that nuptiality only applies to *people* secondarily, but to some aspect of *God* primarily?

So if I am going to argue for procreation as lying at the center of the nuptial mystery, then somehow I must argue that what is "mysterious" in it lies in the purposes of the *given*, not that which lies beyond the given. I shall do this in three stages: first, I will argue that the nuptial mystery applies to human flesh, not to some non-fleshly quality of reality—of relation or virtue or what have you. Second, I shall claim that the flesh of the nuptial mystery must have a history, and thereby be a *differentiated* flesh, a flesh that must somehow struggle in time, for that is what "differentiation" means, metaphysically with respect to the created world. And, finally, I will argue that this differentiation in history that is required by the nuptial mystery, *is* in fact the history of procreation. An attempt to locate some of these remarks within larger systematic concerns will follow, although I need to be candid in admitting that, in all the elements of this argument, my own reflections rely on only partial textual arguments, chosen as *entrées* to the topic, not as full expositions.

At issue is how marital love is shaped by the requirements and vocation of the "public" realities of social formation in families. Although the 1543 *King's Book* already provides an alternative reordering of the "goods of marriage," with "mutual aid and comfort" listed first, there is little sense that this way of framing the list should be read as theological.

THE MYSTERY OF HUMAN FLESH

First, then, I shall have to say something about why the reference to "Christ and the Church" cannot mean that human marriage is symbolic of something beyond itself, but that its meaning can only lie within itself, there, where also we will find Christ and the Church. This must necessarily go against a basic way that the nuptial mystery has been construed over the past few decades at least. For instance, there has been much recent talk of marriage's meaning as bound to its embodiment of some particular or particular group of virtues and relationships that are primarily indicated in Christ's love for the Church: "constancy," for instance, or fidelity, or self-giving.[4] More particularly, much interest has been expressed in regarding marriage as somehow expressing the life of *God*'s own being as Trinity, wherein a certain kind of love between the triune Persons provides both the form and goal of the married state and that is specifically and more primarily expressed in Christ's relationship to the Church. This trinitarian sense of human marriage has had several sources. I would mention only one, and that is the highly influential, though quite short, 1966 book by the Eastern Orthodox theologian Paul Evdokimov entitled *Sacrament of Love*.[5] In some cases where the trinitarian analogy of the origin of human marriage is upheld, the argument then proceeds in this direction: if fidelity and trinitarian love form the mystery of marriage, then it is reasonable to expect that this mystery can be apprehended and even lived in something other than marriage itself, or that whatever is faithful and loving in relationship terms can partake of the mystery of marriage. "Mystery," in this sense, is the symbolically apprehended transference of Christ–Church marriage *qualities* to other situations, including, but not exhaustive of, human marriages. Wherever we see the qualities of Christ's love for the Church expressed, there we see the marriage "mystery."

This general approach seems wrongheaded to me, because it is not how the word "mystery" is used in Scripture, not least by Paul. For Paul, a mystery is not a symbolic dynamic that is discernible in diverse situations. Rather, a mystery is a providential reality unveiled in history: it is a body, as it were, waiting to be disclosed and finally seen in the world; it is a

---

4. See, e.g., A. K. M. Adam, "Disciples Together, Constantly," in *Homosexuality and Christian Community*, ed. Chung-Leong Seow (Louisville: Westminster John Knox, 1996) 123–32.

5. Paul Evdokimov, *The Sacrament of Love: The Nuptial Mystery in the Light of the Orthodox Tradition* (Crestwood, NY: St. Vladimir's Seminary Press, 1985) esp. 105–30.

body that is aimed at bodies. So, at the end of Romans, Paul speaks of the "revelation of the mystery which was kept secret for long ages but is now disclosed and through the prophetic writings is made known to all nations," *viz.* the bringing about the obedience of faith among the Gentiles (Rom 16:25–27). At the opening of Ephesians, he speaks of the "mystery" of "God's will," which aims at the "gathering" of all things in God, and which is "now made known" to Paul (Eph 1:9). In Colossians, Paul refers to the "mystery" of "Christ among" the Gentiles (Col 1:27). In 1 Timothy, the "mystery" is given as something now "confessed": Christ is "manifested in the flesh, vindicated in the Spirit, seen by angels, preached among the nations, believed on in the world, taken up in glory" (1 Tim 3:16)—Christ given over to the Gentiles, that is, and embracing the world. In light of this quite consistent usage of the term, the "mystery" referred to "Christ and the Church" in Ephesians 5 is rightly explicated in *this* sense: God's plan to "draw all men to myself" (John 12:32), through his death on the cross. And the "mystery" of man and woman joined in one flesh—the nuptial mystery—is given in the fact that it is *continuous* with this exposed will of God that gives rise to the Incarnation, crucifixion, and resurrection. "This is a great mystery," Paul writes of male–female marriage, and, literally, he is not saying "and human marriage *really means* Christ and the church." He is saying, this mystery of man and woman joined in one flesh is explicated in, counted among, leads towards, gives rise to, and is bound over for Christ and the Church, Jesus born and given over to hands of men and women for the sake of the world. The mystery is historical, and thereby the contingencies of man and woman are redemptive time's necessity. Or, put another way, apart from human marriage, there is no Christ, no Israel, no body of the nations joined to the Lord's flesh. The "mystery" to which Paul refers is the same as "the book of the genealogy of Jesus Christ, the son of David, the son of Abraham" which opens the Good News; to know the "mystery" of Ephesians 5, we must read the opening verses of Matthew's Gospel.

Now I know that I am being a little contrarian here. We are aware of a long tradition of marriage metaphors or even symbolic or spiritual realities: the Church as Bride, the soul as Bride, the monk or nun as Bride to Christ. And if human marriage is "really about" such symbolic and spiritual realities, then indeed concrete human relations work "down the analogical ladder" as Eugene Rogers likes to say, from something "more real," more divine, and *only then* find some fleshly, limited, human form;

and this tumbling down the ladder could cascade in any number of directions. Everything, in theory, would participate in God's "nuptial reality" if it somehow expressed that reality's supra-physical qualities. But I am suggesting something different—not exactly contradictory, but at least differently ordered. I am suggesting that the body question comes first and that marriages of men and women found the mystery of Christ and the Church—indeed the mystery is that they go together at all, human flesh giving rise to and engaging in the Christic relation, intimately and ultimately; that the Lord Jesus Christ has a genealogy, however odd and disrupted.

Interestingly, when Augustine writes about the nuptial mystery, he will speak, not first in terms of the "mystical" coupling of Christ and his Church, or of the soul and God, or of God and the Son, or of whatever other divine relations might obtrude into our adorations. Rather, Augustine speaks first of the fundamental joining of God the Son and human flesh in the Incarnation.[6] Augustine does not do away with the traditional notion of a marriage of ecclesial Bride and divine Bridegroom. But he wants to stress that this is only the case, in time, in history, because God first took *human* flesh and thereby became "one flesh" with human life. And so he says, "*there*—in the flesh of Christ—was the Bride joined to the Bridegroom in the flesh" (Homily on 1 John 2:2; cf. Sermon 88.7; see also Homily on St. John 8:4). "The nuptial union," Augustine writes on Psalm 45, "is that of 'the Word,' and the flesh. The Bride-chamber of this union [is] the Virgin's womb. For the flesh itself was united to the Word: whence also it is said, 'Henceforth they are not two but one flesh.' [. . .] The Church was assumed unto Him out of the human race: so that the Flesh itself, being united to the Word, might be the Head of the Church: and the rest who believe, members of that Head" (on Psalm 45:3).

---

6. One of the few examinations of this unusual perception is in Claude Chevasse's classic *The Bride of Christ: An Enquiry into the Nuptial Element in Early Christianity* (London: Religious Book Club, 1939) 135–58. Oddly, other readers of the key text of Augustine's exposition of Psalm 45 do not comment on this or do not find it interesting. Cf. David G. Hunter, "The Virgin, the Bride, and the Church: Reading Psalm 45 in Ambrose, Jerome, and Augustine," *Church History* 69 (2000) 281–303. Translations above are by Cleveland Coxe, *Nicene and Post-Nicene Fathers*, vol. 8 (Peabody: Hendrickson, 1994). Chevasse, of course, was hardly alone in noting Augustine's claim, clear and repeated as it is. Yet it tended to be swallowed up in, by serving the interests of, the implications of ecclesial Catholicism, rather than framing the fundamental truth itself of infleshedness. Cf. Gustave Martelet, *The Church's Holiness and Religious Life* (St. Louis: Review for Religious, 1966) 27–32, with references.

For Augustine, who comes back to this theme in many different places, the issue at stake in such "nuptial union" is that "it behooved Christ to suffer and to rise again the third day." *This* reality is something, he says, that is the kernel of the entire gospel, the one thing to be remembered from all the Scriptures (Homily II.2 on 1 John). That is, the purpose of the Christ's incarnational "marriage" was so that God could have a body, a body by which to live within the world, to suffer and die within the world, and in which to be raised to glory. Forsaking "father"—his divine life itself—and "mother"—Jewish Israel's "old types" according to Augustine—Jesus is "born" into the flesh and traverses its paths and edges, for the sake of redeeming those born into the world (see Sermon 41.7). And only *from* this union, as it were, derives the Church, understood to be the vast and unfolding extent of the nations, the "fruit" of his own flesh, since they are part of his "body." Now, of course, all things exist in the *Word*, even before they are "works" within the *world*. But by the Word taking flesh, married as one to the flesh, the works of the Word, like children, people the earth, and the Word's own flesh multiplies within the nations, reaching to the ends of the globe (cf. Ps 45:5, 19, 24, 27; also Ps 19:6).

For Augustine, to speak of marriage is to speak only secondarily of the nuptial mystery of "Christ and the Church," insofar as the Church is Christ's "body" only in a secondary sense compared to Christ's historical flesh born, crucified, and risen. And to this extent, Augustine's focus upon Jesus's *own* earthly body as the locus of marriage is not only unusual but challenging.[7] But, interestingly, Psalm 45 was traditionally appointed for the feast days of the Nativity in the West, both in the Roman and Sarum rites (from which it passed into the Lectionary of the sixteenth-century *Book of Common Prayer*). Still, and despite these liturgical assertions, the notion of the marriage "mystery" as being *about* fleshiness here, as its "oneness" is described in terms of a "passion" of suffering, rather than first about a quality of a relation, is not commonly articulated.[8]

7. The interest in the Church as "body" to Jesus' "head" is a main point of Augustine's exegesis; but this goes in a quite different direction from other commentators on, e.g., Psalm 45, like Ambrose and Jerome, who use the psalm to makes points regarding the superiority of virginity to the married state. For Augustine, it is the fact that we have bodies at all, that we are creatures in a world needing redemption and to which Jesus comes with his own body, that is at issue. There are no "elites" whether married, widowed, or virgin. Rather, it is membership in the Body of Christ that allows one to be brought to Christ. But he is the "first fruits" of this Body, given in the Eucharist (Homily on 1 John 2:2).

8. Psalm 45 is used liturgically on Christmas Day in the Roman, Sarum, and English rites, on Annunciation in the Gregorian, or Psalm 19 on Christmas Day Matins. Hebrews

THE MYSTERY OF FLESH'S HISTORY

But it was never wholly lost sight of either, at least subliminally. So now I want to press its implications theologically, because they lead more directly back to the scriptural understanding of marriage's more concretely procreative center. If Augustine's insight makes any sense—that is, that the mystery of marriage lies in the incarnate body through which Jesus suffers for the sake of reaching the nations—then is it any surprise that the more specifically *sexual* character of Jesus's body should be a matter of concern for Christians? In one of those classic kinds of texts that make you reorient your ways of seeing things, the art critic Leo Steinberg created a stir in the early 1980s with a deliberately provocative argument claiming that the sexual identity of Jesus was quite specifically a matter of intense interest to Christians in the later Middle Ages and Renaissance.[9] In spite of some ecclesial warnings to the contrary, and perhaps under the partial influence of Franciscan piety, depictions of Jesus from the thirteenth century through to the middle of the sixteenth century show an increasing and often shocking focus on his genitalia. This is so in paintings and sculpture dealing with his infancy through to his crucifixion, death, and ascension. In image after image, Jesus's penis is pointed at, fondled, celebrated, wreathed with flowers, rosaries, and rich garments; it is exposed, emphasized, erected, and flagged with garments whipped up by the Spirit's wind. Part of Steinberg's purpose in detailing this coherent iconography was simply to get people to admit to what was always before their eyes as they have, for centuries, gazed at pictures by Cranach, del Piombo, Veronese, Dürer, and others; and in admitting to this, grapple honestly with *why* Christians would embrace such iconographic risk so consistently and openly.[10] What were they

---

1:8–9 uses Psalm 45 messianically and, to that extent contextually, incarnationally. See also Seikle Greidjanus, *Menschwording en vernedering, Diss.* (Wageningen: Vada, 1903) xxiv. Nicholas Cabasilas, in his *The Life in Christ* (Crestwood, NY: St. Vladimir's Seminary Press, 1974) 123–24, speaks more generally of marriage with the "flesh," using Genesis 2 as his basis, in reference to the incarnational basis for *theiosis* via the Eucharist.

9. Leo Steinberg, *The Sexuality of Christ in Renaissance Art and in Modern Oblivion* (Chicago: University of Chicago Press, 1996).

10. There were many critics, mostly art historians, who strongly objected to Steinberg's thesis, largely on the basis that there is hardly any documented evidence that Christian iconographers had any theological intent in framing their images of Jesus in this manner. At the same time, these critics could not answer the "why" question very coherently, especially in the face of an otherwise disconcerting pattern of representation. Steinberg's first task, therefore, was to get us to *see* the images clearly, and only then to seek theological rationale; to overcome avoidance so as to grapple with mean-

saying? I turn to Steinberg's arguments, not because they are exhaustive in explaining the Christian tradition on these matters, but as a useful doorway through which to engage this tradition.

Steinberg analyzes three main purposes to these popular paintings:

a. The first was to draw into historical coherence the kind of life God in fact assumed: that is, one in which life struggles against its extermination. For traditional Christian homiletic explication, and iconography as a result, mortality is correlative with sexuality. Why do we have sex? In order to have children. And why have children? Because we die, and only through our sexual operations shall humanity and, if only vaguely, something of ourselves, somehow survive. These are themes commonly expounded by well-rehearsed teachers like Gregory the Great and Bede. They are theological themes, but also ones that are deeply resonant with simple human instincts as they are integrated into Christian teaching. God's "humanation" therefore, in Steinberg's words, demands "the condition of being both deathbound and sexed" (15). Jesus must be joined to the struggle to survive in the face of the darkness. And so the pictures (explicated by homilies laying out the narrative details) of Mary's diaphanous head-veil cloaking both her infant son's genitals at birth, and later offering them a similar protection as he hangs upon the Cross. As the Franciscan *Meditations* of Pseudo-Bonaventure state, here, in the veiling of his genitalia, we have a premonition of death even in birth, now bound to the flesh the Lord assumes (30ff.). Death and sex are well understood in their inextricable bonds long before Freud (or Woody Allen).

b. The second reason to emphasize that Jesus had a penis, according to Steinberg, is to remind us of the fact that Jesus himself redeemed the application of human sexuality by his own chastity (18). No modern Whitmanesque *celebration* of sweaty erotic ardor here; simply the declaration that the *incarnate* God bore the use of his organ virtuously. In the pertinent words of the medieval author Bernardus Silvestris, "Unconquered, the nuptial weapons fight with death, they restore nature and perpetuate the race" (46). "Unconquered," chastity, that is, is not the enemy of procreation—nor is Jesus—but is the means

---

ing. His speculated meanings are arguable, perhaps; but only within a context willing to admit to the representations themselves. To date, alternative theories, on this basis, have not proved as coherent as his own. Steinberg answers his critics fulsomely in the second edition of the book.

by which its purpose is rightly channeled. Amid the many theological discussions over whether the resurrected Jesus still bore his circumcised penis, the most assertive answer was in the positive: surely he would, for it is a *signum victoriae*, a sign of victory (86). We might note that the category of "virginity" as a Christian calling rightly falls as a subset of this reality (at least in this reading), and not as a primary category itself. Virginity marks the victory over sexuality's perverted fall, not over sexuality itself, and it thereby marks the direction that sexual life is moving in God's eschatological summation of all things. It is itself a *signum*, not a fulfillment.

c. Finally, the depictions of Jesus's genitalia during this period indicate how the unashamed *pudenda* of Jesus mark the redemption of shame itself and the renewal of innocence (19ff.). That is, the entire acceptance of a body given over to the mortal struggle of every man and woman of the race was itself, in all of its mortal suffering, the assumption by God of sexual demand and agony, and of its fruit. Hence, we can understand the late-medieval and Renaissance interest in depicting (and preaching on) Jesus's circumcision (which is hardly one of today's homiletic obsessions), for circumcision is the mark of his maleness and, within the Law's framework, the testimony to the promises of human generation, drawn into correspondence with his death. Linked to this are the many paintings in which the blood from the side of the dying or dead Jesus is ineluctably drawn down to the place of his circumcision, often with glaring focus. In the teaching of the exegetes, Jesus's circumcision as an infant stood as a kind of sacrificial "guarantee" of his future death, his "first blood" as it was sometimes put, or, in the words of the seventeenth-century English poet Richard Crashaw, "first fruit of my growing death" (47). Multiple are the images of the dead Christ, lamentations over his corpse, even depictions of the throne of Grace in which the Father holds the mortally wounded son upon his lap like a Pietà, with Jesus pointing to his own genitalia—the *signum victoriae* to be sure, but now revealed as such only through the work of sacrifice. Sex is bloody and bloodied for the sake of life.

By the sixteenth-century's latter half, as movements of moral reform within the Roman Church gained steam, we see a retreat from these kinds of images, one that was almost complete by the seventeenth century. Within early modernity, as Baroque sensibility unfolds, Jesus is more carefully and completely clothed, the indicating and symbolic features regarding his private parts are eliminated, and, in Steinberg's phrase, "the sexuality of Christ" is consigned to a kind of "modern oblivion." I would go on and add that the issue of human sexuality becomes instead more of a *secular* affair, and the issue of Christ more of a *spiritual* one. Interestingly, this has set the course of much modern theological interest: Christologies tend to become more adoptionist, the Holy Spirit becomes the key to joining or raising the human Jesus to God, and the flesh becomes a kind of instrument to be pneumatically wielded. Already in the seventeenth century Milton rebelled (quite understandably, I might add) against his own unhappy union by redefining human marriage as "mystical," that is, redefining the nuptial mystery itself, and arguing that only when marriage can be the actual full embodiment of true "soul love" is its meaning accomplished. Instead of a struggle for continued life against the mixed motives of a fallen world grasped by redemptive sacrifice, "sincerity" of feeling and motive now becomes the test of nuptiality, no more.[11] And so we ask of any couple *before* they are married, "do you love each other?" as if it is this feeling towards the other that is of the essence, while marriage itself provides only a form (perhaps one of many available forms) in which the essence can be enacted in time.

My favorite exemplar of this modern attitude in its flowering development, American poet Walt Whitman, still casts his shadow widely. Theology in both academy and Church is written within his penumbra: bodies are important, but they are important because of what they *signify*—love, desire, play, gratuity, freedom—not because of what they simply are: creaturely stuff that God has made, that has come into being, that is beset by the crushing weight of time, that struggles through its varied duties, and gives itself away, happily or not, into God's hands for remaking. It is because someone like Whitman had no christological framework in which to order creation, that created matter required an alternative canonization of its givenness, now viewed in terms of its affective embrace: what is, must and can only be enjoyed. Bodies today would prefer to be the playthings of the Spirit, where "Spirit" stands for guaranteed of bare "isness," not that which stands over and against the Spirit, as they had always seemed to be, a place wherein incarnation spilled necessarily its blood for the sake of God's own ordering of time.

---

11. See Witte, *From Sacrament to Contract*, 183–84.

The feminist question—how can a male body save a female one—which has been answered in terms of Gal 3:28 ("in Christ there is neither male nor female"), represents a confusion of categories here. While God, in Christ, may take up male and female equally in his salvific purpose and grace, this spiritual promise does *not* change the status of bodies themselves, which are male or female and which must still find their place within a world whose own contours scrape against the contours of each one's distinct physicality. In this historical context, it is the particularity of the Law that governs Jesus's maleness, that demands his circumcision, that fights against his chastity, that draws his blood from the particularity of his flesh, and that thereby orders his place within the *history* of Jewish genealogy. The life of God in the world of flesh issues from these realities, is attacked by them, resists their finally destructive forces, and in the end, sweeps them up.[12]

So, for Augustine, even in the secondary character of the nuptial mystery as the joining of Christ to the Church, Bridegroom to Bride, the point he wants to make is that, from whatever perspective one chooses to view this, the "marriage" is, as it were, between that which is utterly *different*: divinity and human flesh, male and female, Jew and Gentile. Whose family is the Gentiles' after all? he asks: the Devil's! It is from Satan's body that the nations are wrenched into the nuptials of their Jewish Lord![13] Sexual differentiation is bound to the realities of sin and death confronted by love and redemption, not because bodies and sex are bad or ugly, but because this is the history of human flesh—its distinct bodies, often impossible resolutions, stumblings, struggle, loss, death, and redemption. To get from one place to another in time, from one moment to another, from creation to redemption, from creature to Redeemer, one must pass through this history of beleaguered propagation. And although we might wish to ask "why?"—why is divine love *this*

---

12. The claim that when Paul says in several places that there is "no *x* or *y* in Christ" (male, female, slave, free, Jew, Greek, etc.) we are being presented with a work of Christ that does away with created distinctions is clearly absurd, on Paul's own terms. It cannot be a matter of erasing distinctions, otherwise Romans 9–11 would be pointless. Rather, it is a question of being saved *within* the distinctiveness of Christ: all have sinned, all are consigned to disobedience, and all, in their distinctiveness, are saved in Christ. What Christ does is itself a *different* work than the work of "distinguishing" in Genesis 1. But it is not a work that denies or contradicts Genesis 1. The fact there are "no circumcised or uncircumcised" does not do away with circumcision, but rather puts all into the circumcision of Christ in his flesh, as in Col 2:11.

13. On Ps 45; see also *City of God* 17.16.

love and not another?—and although we may be able even to provide fitting answers, yet even apart from our questions and responses, the history itself is inevitable.

Nuptiality cannot, therefore, be mainly about "difference" as a principle, the love of "the other" in general, the looking at another as he or she is perceiving *us*, as Rowan Williams has said, or the "hermeneutics" of such nuptial mutual giving.[14] The nuptial "difference" that founds its "mystery" is not a principle, but applies always to *particulars*: a dog, not a cat; a fish, not a clam; a cow, not a pig; a locust, not a fly; a circumcision, not an androgyn. And as particulars, they are particulars in time that moves from one moment to another, and that is permitted so to move, and that has within itself the motive of its temporal sustenance. "But when the time had fully come, God sent forth his Son, born of a woman, born under the law, to redeem those who were under the law" (Gal 4:4f). The male–female distinction given within the created "image of God" mentioned in Gen 1:27, and of which much has been made, is not about union as such ("unitivity"), as if the matter concerns "coming together" or "mutuality" or "complementarity," although all this may be at work. Rather, the *imago* is about the *history* of a union, of a coming together. It is about how it happens, and what it takes, and what comes from it. After all, the true "image of God" is the Son himself (2 Cor 4:4; Col 1:15; Heb 1:3; John 1:18), and, as the Letter to the Hebrews lays it out *in toto*, it is the "character" of the image to have a story, a passage—creating, speaking, taking flesh, being tempted, sacrificing, pioneering, going through the heavens, entering glory. The *imago* is given in terms of "days" (Heb 1:2). If the male–female distinction is essential—and it *is*—it is essential in *this* way, *this* movement, wherein God creates what is not Him, and sends His Son to die within it, so that "he might bring many sons to glory" (Heb 2:10).

THE MYSTERY OF PROCREATION'S TIME

The procreative character of marriage emerges from this temporal movement of God's providential care. It is certainly not inappropriate to take concepts like "difference" and "otherness" and "mutual self-giving" and the like, as well as the kind of "love" that might express or embody these

---

14. Cf. David McCarthy Matzko, "The Relationship of Bodies: A Nuptial Hermeneutics of Same-Sex Unions," *Theology and Sexuality* 4 (1998) 96–112. This is not to rule out such elements as informing nuptiality, but they can be so only secondarily, as aspects of something more fundamental.

things, and then to say that somehow these qualities adhere to and even to some extent help explicate what the nuptial mystery is. For all these elements also describe in a real way the character of God's relational love for us. It is not inappropriate to use these concepts in this way, but it is easily misleading, and requires a rigorous discipline of reference. But is it appropriate that these terms, as it were, *drive* their reference into the "whole wide world," so that all that gives itself in difference and mutuality and loving freedom and so on is therefore also expressive of the nuptial mystery, including a range of relational loves that might even embrace same-sex unions? The answer is "no." It is not appropriate because the self-giving love into difference that is God's has a particular *history*, not a general character. Such love as this *creates bodies and new bodies again*, and it does so within the framework of struggle by which the creation of new bodies is a necessary challenge, not an irrelevance. And if not irrelevant but necessary, one cannot think that the divine statement "be fruitful and multiply" is *not* itself intrinsic to the *imago* just described in the Genesis text—male and female he created them in his own image (Gen 1:27, 28). For God creates, and the image of that creation—its history—is one of struggle, both of male and female together, toiling and anguishing in childbirth, yet being bound to one another; it is the image of the God whose embrace of such a flesh as this arises out of just such a toiling and anguishing and desiring, and leads just to a cross where mothers weep and abandonment is felt. The image of God is life-giving—that is, procreative—and that is the image in which male and female find their place in union. It is true that this or that individual may love the particularities of this or that body, give oneself over to it and receive from it—gay or straight. But the character of the specifically *nuptial* mystery is quite specific with regard to particular loves: it is that in this giving there be the history of struggle, fraught though it may be with death, to give life.[15]

Bodies are life-bearing. That is the key to the entire anthropology of the Scriptures. And when Paul cries out, "who shall deliver me from this body of death?" (Rom 7:24), he is not denying this fact, or announcing its overturning for some New Age (though some have wrongly thought so) or

15. Versus Eugene Rogers, in his response to Bernd Wannenwetsch, in "The Liturgical Body," *Modern Theology* 16 (2000) 370–71. It is not "particularity" itself that is at issue here—particular bodies, particular forms, particular desires—all of which, as Rogers rightly points out, apply to any act of love among particular people. The particularity of love is not a principle that explains the nuptial mystery. Rather, what is at issue are the *particulars* involved in such a mystery.

pronouncing a judgment on something that simply cannot be. He is declaring quite simply, and in tandem with his entire vision of the Law, that what is designed for life now creeps about in the shadow of that which crushes life. Do we not know this also? He is taking into his cry the anguish of childbirth, which, not until the mid-nineteenth century at least (and only in some places, and today too not in every place), was the site of countless deaths. He is taking in the uncontrollable bleeding of mothers, the diseases of childhood, the slaughtering of innocents, the murders of brothers, the violence of men, the bitter infertilities and barrenness, the wars and famines of Jerusalem's rubble, the sword that pierces a mother's heart (Luke 2:35). Bodies are life-bearing, even and especially in the face of death. And something like the whole book of Leviticus—with its interest in fluids and scabs and menstruation and moldy houses and homesteads and fathers and mothers and sisters and aunts and yes, sex itself—this grand Book of Blood that rises up in the New Testament as the Sacrifice of Christ, the son of Mary, is but a comment on the body's birth. If, in a phrase Rowan Williams has made well-known, the body has a "grace," it is in the first place the grace of being born and giving birth, and the grace too of facing into its own loss and incapacities as well. This is its love; not something prior to it or other than it.[16]

The notion that procreation is not at the center of scriptural anthropology, let alone the nuptial mystery has, as I mentioned earlier, had some of its most recent roots in something misleadingly attributed to a recapturing of Eastern Orthodox attitudes. Those like Paul Evdokimov or Olivier Clément,[17] who has followed him on this particular topic, have insisted that children cannot be at the center of marriage's meaning and purpose because they are so self-evidently contingent in reception—infertility being the most obvious reason this might be the case. At best, Evdokimov and others have argued, children emerge from marriages as visible signs of the "superabundance" of love between the partners (and

---

16. The title to Williams's now-famous essay, "The Body's Grace," derives, as he explains it, from Paul Scott's novel *The Day of the Scorpion*, and describes one of the novel's characters who, after having been seduced, and despite her ambivalence, has finally recognized how she has "entered her body's grace." What seems problematic with Williams's argument is precisely the logical ordering of its recognitions, that is, that one might properly explore the body's "grace" first from the experience of sexual pleasure, which might, in itself, somehow provide the foundation for an understanding of the graciousness of physicality.

17. Olivier Clément, *Corps de mort et de gloire: Petite intoduction à une théopoetique du corps* (Paris: Desclée de Brouwe, 1995) 81–101.

there may be other signs as well). But it is love, understood in particular ways, that, according to Evdokimov, defines procreation, not the other way around. Indeed, Evdokimov claimed—and this has been one of the elements of his discussion that has attracted many—such love is properly seen as reflective of the Trinity's own inner life, between Father, Son, and Spirit, and it is *this* that marriage represents, not the multiplication of bodies.

I need to digress here, somewhat polemically, because Evdokimov's work has been used as a frequently cited buttress to non-procreative arguments, including those of same-sex marriage proponents like Eugene Rogers.[18] In fact, the notion that there is an "alternative Eastern Orthodox" understanding of marriage that somehow avoids Western and "Augustinian pessimism" about the body, to which the tradition's emphasis on procreative centrality is attributed, represents an aspect of imaginative self-redefinition on the part of an innovative group of twentieth-century French-Russian Orthodox émigrés. Their conclusions have often been wielded in the pursuit of anti-Roman Catholic polemics and in eccentric theological speculation, or both.[19] I admire Evdokimov enormously on a number of scores, but not here: he misapplies (and one must think he did so deliberately, given his vast knowledge) Patristic sources, of which there were few he can deduce in any case, to make his tendentious point. And he himself gets caught up with ideas of androgyns, feminine "poles" to God and reality, and related topics whose historically Gnostic relatives have always sat uneasily with the broader Christian tradition.[20] A glance at Eastern Orthodox marriage *liturgies*, in

18. Rogers, *Sexuality and the Christian Body*, 72–85, 190–96, 206–8, 211–17, *et passim*. While Evdokimov does not figure so explicitly in Rogers's later work on the Holy Spirit, his influence stands in the shadow and continues to exert a strong pull. Cf. Rogers' *After the Spirit: A Constructive Pneumatology from Resources outside the Modern West* (Grand Rapids: Eerdmans, 2005) 188. Rogers's pneumatology, although its reach extends much farther (and in many creative ways) than sexuality, is nonetheless still caught up in the relational aspects of divine life that drive his reflections in his earlier book.

19. The kind of distorted anti-Westernism to which Evdokimov's ideas have been crudely applied, without Patristic investigation, is well illustrated in, e.g., Clifford Stevens, "The Trinitarian Roots of the Nuptial Community," *St. Vladimir's Theological Quarterly* 35 (1991) 351–58.

20. See William Basil Zion, *Eros and Transformation: Sexuality and Marriage; an Eastern Orthodox Perspective* (Lanham, MD: University Press of America, 1992) 137–71. Nor is Zion exactly an enemy of Evdokimov's views here, but he shows how Evdokimov sought to reframe Patristic thinking, in a completely ahistorical way, in the service of a larger and more idiosyncratic vision. To be fair, Rogers himself alludes to these distortions, though he does not seem constrained by this knowledge. See Rogers, *Sexuality and the Christian Body*, 73–74.

any case, reveals that they are highly procreative in focus.[21] This is not to say that there are no differences in tone between Eastern and Western Christian emphases here. Rather, the problem for Christian East and West together, though in different ways, was that the Old Testament realities with respect to the human body were so conclusively set aside exegetically, in favor of spiritualizing readings of the scriptural texts. Again, the implicit and often explicit Marcionite character of modern Christianity, both Western *and* Eastern, stands behind much of the deformation in understanding of the nuptial mystery.

It was Eusebius, long ago and in the wake of the Christian Church's final triumph over the powers of paganism (or so it seemed), who clearly made the distinction:[22] although Jews may well have needed to propagate their religion in the midst of an evil world through bearing and raising children, now that the gospel is given, and the world is "perishing" and winding down within its glorious light, virginity and childlessness well befit the Christian Church, just as the Spirit follows the Law. And Eusebius was simply providing a historical elucidation to a long-standing Christian bias in favor of virginity or at least "chastity" in the face of the end of the world and the need to live without "encumbrances." Tertullian (and others) had long before driven home the point that having children was no virtue for a Christian seeking to divest her- or himself of the world's things so as better to die naked and freely in and for the Lord:

> And marrying, let us be overtaken by the last day, like Sodom and Gomorrah; that day when the "woe" pronounced over "such as are with child and giving suck" shall be fulfilled, that is, over the married and the incontinent: for from marriage result wombs, and breasts, and infants. And when an end of marrying? I believe after the end of living![23]

Though Tertullian saw martyrdom as the appropriate and, hopefully, soon "end of living," his implication was that life in this world at least

---

21. See John Meyendorff, *Marriage: An Orthodox Perspective* (Crestwood, NY: St. Vladimir's Seminary Press, 1984) 113–31. The Liturgies of Betrothal and Crowning (included in the English translation of Evdokimov's *Sacrament of Love*, 130–48) are infused by a central procreative concern, deeply rooted in the historical and genealogical unfolding of Israel's service to the human race.

22. Eusebius *Demonstratio Evangelica* (Proof of the gospel) I.9.

23. Tertullian *On Chastity* c. 11.

presupposes "wombs, breasts, and infants," that is, childbearing, much as it disgusts and disappoints him.

Augustine, by contrast (and hardly "pessimistically" with regard to historical existence) continues to see "fruitfulness" as a key Christian reality that is exposed to light within human marriage. Cautiously taking his stand against Jerome's ascetically oriented, anti-marriage views, Augustine explains that the "sacramental" character of marriage is given in the still necessary reality of human procreation, as well as in procreation's genealogical figure, that is, the gathering in of the Gentiles.[24] Procreation and Gentile evangelism and baptism are connected, he points out, precisely in the way the first founds the historical reality, in time and in generational reach, of extending the passional life of Jesus into the diverse realm of the nations who are gathered before the throne of God in praise. This, after all, is the image with which the Bible ends, in Revelation (21:12, 24), wherein the Gentiles are matched to Israel's twelve tribes, fulfilling the expressly procreative language of Ezekiel (47:22f.; 48).[25]

Talk of "tribes" and "nations" and "languages" is precisely talk of "species." Indeed, within the grip of the Fall and of human sin universalized, the scriptural discussion of the "tribes" of the world is the original talk of "endangered species." The reason we translate Bibles into hundreds of languages is not only to share the gospel with all "kinds" of

---

24. Augustine *De bono conjugali* (On the Good of Marriage) 21. Augustine, to be sure, is not averse to the notion of changing procreative demands in different dispensations. The greater need for children in the time of the Patriarchs is one reason he adduces for the divine permission of polygamy (17).

25. Tertullian's own acerbic wit is put to use on this topic, from the ironic viewpoint of the heretic, as he addresses Marcion's argument against marriage and sexual (procreative) engagement: "To put a complete stop, however, to the sowing of the human race, may, for anything I know, be quite consistent for Marcion's most good and excellent god. For how could he desire the salvation of man, whom he forbids to be born, when he takes away that institution from which his birth arises? How will he find any one on whom to set the mark of his goodness, when he suffers him not to come into existence? How is it possible to love him whose origin he hates? Perhaps he is afraid of a redundant population, lest he should be weary in liberating so many; lest he should have to make many heretics; lest Marcionite parents should produce too many noble disciples of Marcion. The cruelty of Pharaoh, which slew its victims at their birth, will not prove to be more inhuman in comparison. For while he destroyed lives, our heretic's god refuses to give them: the one removes from life, the other admits none to it. There is no difference in either as to their homicide—man is slain by both of them; by the former just after birth, by the latter as yet unborn. Thanks should we owe you, you god of our heretic, had you only checked the dispensation of the Creator in uniting male and female; for from such a union indeed has your Marcion been born!" (*Against Marcion*, I.29, transl. P. Holmes, in *Ante-Nicene Fathers* vol. 3 [Peabody: Hendrickson, 1994] 294–95).

people, but to protect the "endangered species" of these kinds and the human kind as a whole. It is interesting in this context that someone like Rogers will argue that procreation is a species-limited concern, not an individual—including individual marriage—concern. Indeed, if there was in fact a command to "fill the earth" given to Adam and Eve, who would deny that the earth is already filled? So, says Rogers in a modern, demographically retooled Eusebian fashion, procreation serves no central purpose any longer. "The earth is now more or less full."[26] Although I am not sure what "more or less full" means, it is certainly the case that it is just the "species," or, more properly in the New Testament, the "genus" (offspring, generation, nation, kind) that is at issue in the redemptive history of Christ, from Jew to Greek, from Sinai to Pentecost, from First Adam to Second Adam. Is there something peculiarly "Jewish" about such an interest? Not at all. In fact, the true politics of responsibility, what makes politics both possible and necessary, derives from a recognition that procreative and species-oriented understandings of the nuptial mystery are central to its truth as a divine gift. It is a sorry misconstrual of creation that believes that an anti-procreative anthropology

26. Rogers, *Sexuality and the Christian Body*, 206. Rogers appeals to Aquinas, in part, for his argument, on the basis that Thomas links the good of procreation to the propagation of the *species* primarily, something that, once completed in theory, would free the sexual act for other goods. But Thomas (e.g., in the *Summa Theologiae* Ia 98) is more subtle: the existence of *individuals* is not separable from the species, and hence procreation is essential to the individual's destiny as well, *qua* individual, and the "natural" purposes of procreative sexual life are bound to a divine "blessing" that is fundamental to the creation of human individuals in their essential historical purpose, regardless of the Fall. Thomas (98.2) is also clear that the sexual distinction of male and female is bound to this procreative purpose. Furthermore, the "helpmeet" character of Adam's need could easily have been met, even *better* met, according to Thomas, by another male! Procreative heterosexual sex is therefore the *essential* meaning of sexual differentiation and the sexual act. (At the same time, Thomas's argument that sexual intercourse itself is independent of the Fall, and, as bound to procreation, would have proceeded "in Paradise" irrespective of the Fall, cannot be taken, as some have, as an argument in favor of sexual pleasure's divine integrity; in 98.2 Thomas, following Augustine, is explicit that intercourse apart from sin is something in which physical desire has no place, or at least is "completely" subject to reason.) In any case, "species" for Thomas seems to stand to the individual human creature in the same way that the Church stands to the individual Christian in Augustine's terms. Rogers' treatment of this question is commended by Princeton ethicist and philosopher Jeffrey Stout in "How Charity Transcends the Culture Wars: Eugene Rogers and Others on Same-Sex Marriage" (*Journal of Religious Ethics* 31 [2003] 170–72), and although I too would second Stout's judgment that Rogers's discussion represents a far more "charitable" approach to the question, in part because openly grappling with the Church's tradition in a constructive rather than simply dismissive way, it must be wondered whether the tools for his revisioning can realistically be found in the tradition with which he engages.

could ever sustain a politics of, say, ecological responsibility, since that to which such an anthropology gives rise is precisely an anti-politics.

To talk procreatively about marriage is to place, once again, the agonistic character of historical redemption—what divine creation is substantively shaped by—back at the center of our vocation. In R. S. Thomas's phrase, marriage takes place "in a world in servitude to time."[27] That is not a matter of its Fall in the first place, but of its nature. I have argued this elsewhere,[28] but the main point is simply to take seriously and essentially the fact that the life-bearing character of the body is, by definition, under threat, by virtue of its created character and doubly so by the corrupted conditions of its history. Thus, the body's procreative mission carries out its passage through time always, as it were, under an assault, though now, taken over by the flesh of Christ Jesus, this assault reveals the redemptive power of God. The issue of marital "love," then, arises from *within* such an agonistic context—it is defined by struggle, by ordering, by self-restraint, by self-offering, by compromise, by risking, by failing, by renewal.

Only from *within* this agonistic context of procreative purpose does the proper discussion of infertile marriages or even celibacy arise. While that is another discussion from the present one, it is, I hope, obvious that it will not do simply to claim that the acceptance of barren marriages by the Church must mean that, say, all inherently sterile relationships are also acceptable. For it is the struggle for and ordering of procreation that makes sense of sterility, not the other way around. It is not that "Christ and the Church" stand "behind" human marriage as a form to a shadow (among many shadows). Rather, Christ and the Church are given to the world through human marriage—they are ontologically connected, because history is the seedbed of human redemption. They cannot be pried apart, conceptually, let alone "in fact." When the New Testament is used, as Jerome and others did, to justify the falling away of the connection between time and sexuality, and therefore as a mandate for virginity over and against the Old Testament witness, the very meaning of celibacy (or sterility for that matter) is undercut. Both find their meaning

---

27. R. S. Thomas, "A Marriage," in *Mass for Hard Times* (Newcastle-Upon-Tyne: Bloodaxe, 1994) 74.

28. Ephraim Radner, *Hope Among the Fragments: The Broken Church and Its Engagement of Scripture* (Grand Rapids: Brazos, 2004) 134–35.

within genealogies, not apart from them; both of these are a *part of,* not an alternative to the agonistic order of procreation.

This ordered struggle has been described in different ways. Chrysostom called the marriage household a "little church" in this regard, and he was hardly being idealistic in such a description.[29] Anglicans, like William Whateley, often spoke of marriage as a "little commonwealth," in deliberate analogy with the body politic of the city or nation.[30] The procreative fruits of a marriage are better seen in this kind of context, than they are explained (or criticized as important) in terms of their linkage to individualized receptacles and authors of desire—who "gets" a child, who does not, who is lucky, who is unlucky, who needs one or does not or should have access to a child and is being denied even though she or he may want one. This is an approach that has taken over modern conceptions of procreation, and wrongly so. Instead, and more properly, the language of duties and responsibilities, of constraints and freedoms, of ordering and reordering, of stops and starts, of commonalities and adjudications, of authorities and subjections, of generosities and impoverishments, of crises and interventions, of peace and flourishing, of structures and stabilities, of edifications and reformations—such language as this describes life over time. Such a life is better viewed as borne in such a "commonwealth" and as shared in such a commonwealth even by the childless, than as some kind of gratuitous or optional surplus attendant to personal desire. If marriage is a means of sanctification, as someone like Rogers rightly argues,[31] it is nonetheless not a means

---

29 John Chrysostom *Homily 20* on Eph 5:22–33, in St. John Chrysostom, *On Marriage and Familiy Life* (Crestwood, NY: St. Vladimir's Seminary Press, 2003) 57. The love of husband and wife is "the force that welds society together" (44). Chrysostom is rightly identified as one of the few early Fathers who considers marriage favorably, and does so at some length in a range of homiletic material. But Chrysostom also ranges widely and inconsistently in his positive arguments. Sometimes heterosexual marriage is primarily about "love" and "attraction" and hence it is the higher analogy of all friendship, like David's and Jonathan's (43–45). Sometimes it is about procreation primarily (74; "the root of our very existence," 76). Sometimes it is about a bridle to fornication in an era when procreation is no longer necessary (81, 85–86). Chrysostom also makes use of the Platonic androgyn model of original Adamic "unity" (75–77) although to different effect than most modern applications of the myth.

30. Whateley, *Directions for Married Persons*, chapter 7. Cf. also John Witte's extensive discussion of this concept within Anglicanism in particular, devoting to the topic an entire chapter, in *From Sacrament to Contract*, 130–93.

31. Rogers, *Sexuality and the Christian Body*, e.g., chapter 3 (67–85) and chapter 13 (269–75). The ascetic character of sexuality's divine purpose is, in fact, the central argument of Rogers's book, and is approached from a variety of perspectives throughout.

given apart from the particularities of the "procreative commonwealth," and thus is not simply transferable to any set of faithful relationships—friendships, same-sex partnerships, and so on.

When Whately begins his treatise on marriage by founding it upon the two primary goods of what he calls "chastity" and "benevolence," it may strike today's Christian as an anachronistic focus on the worn-out virtues of a now fortuitously decrepit social institution. But when he explains that these two elements necessarily found a faithful response to the divine command to *procreate*, one realizes that (and, I would argue, quite rightly) the sexual act, the ordering of the body, is being understood within a context that *must* respond to the givenness of a world where individual choices are fruitful only as they seek out the order that can sustain a family. "Therefore, the man shall leave his father and his mother, and the two shall become one flesh." "One-fleshedness," in terms of the nuptial mystery, is primarily a familial reality, something even Chrysostom, for all his unsystematic reflections, recognized. Just as the marriage of man and woman gives rise to a child drawn from the flesh of each, and thus the child in a sense embodies that single flesh, so, even in cases of infertility, Chrysostom argues, the marriage of man and woman, and their sexual consummation of that marriage, casts a procreative shadow upon time, and holds within its form fruitfulness itself.[32]

My own view, however, is that it is simply not possible to define an "ascetic purpose" in the abstract as indeed a potentially transferable set of disciplines that could be applied to any number of sexually bound relationships. Logically, the historical particulars—in this case the procreative purpose of sexuality given to and through male and female—define what "sanctification" actually means.

32. Chrysostom *Homily 12* on Col 4:18 in St. John Chrysostom, *On Marriage and Family Life*, 75–76. Scripture teaches that mankind was made a little lower than the angels. But when a couple manifests the mystery in their physical union, they are lifted above the angelic hosts and into the realm of the Divine Life. Among all of creation, only human beings are given the power and the responsibility to cooperate with God in *ex nihilo* creation, to bring about a human soul when there once was nothing. Chrysostom points out that "Scripture does not say, 'They shall be one flesh.' But they shall be joined together '*into* one flesh,' namely the child. Chrysostom continues, "As if she were gold receiving purest gold," the wife receives her husband "and within her it is nourished, cherished and refined. It is mingled with her own substance and she then returns it as a child!" And even in the case when a couple is unable to conceive, Chrysostom argues, the sexual consummation of a man and his wife "casts a procreative shadow upon time, and holds within its form, fruitfulness itself." *Eros* can only be called love when it has a goal beyond pleasure. (The Greek text of Matt 19:5 reads, *kai esontai hoi duo eis sarka mian*, literally "and the two shall be with/in one flesh"). My thanks to Matthew Olver for this point.

THEOLOGY AND PROCREATION

I end my discussion now by moving to a consideration of the theological or systematic context for the nuptial mystery's procreative center. I do this in order more properly to locate the discussion of marriage in today's inescapable disputes. I began my reflections with the general claim that the nuptial mystery is mysterious, not because there is something to which marriage points *beyond* its own flesh. Marriage doesn't mean anything beyond its own history, and is not significant because of what lies *behind* it, so that if you could discover it, having abstracted this "something" (desire, mutuality, relationship, sacrifice, delight, self-opening), you might be able to discern it or even apply it to other human realities, perhaps even identify it in some primordially divine context. This abstracting and reapplication is precisely what is at issue in current disputes about marriage, especially within the Church. And, of course, there are plenty of realities that *do* lie beyond and behind marriage—God himself, for instance. So, is there no intrinsic connection between human marriage and, say, the very nature and life of God? Let us, therefore, reflect more generally about this very pertinent question that, as I mentioned, lies at the heart of so much current disagreement.

The fundamental constraint on human love, within the context of the life-bearing vocation of human bodies, is that it is enacted within a vast realm of ignorance. That is one essential element in the reality of bodies in time, whether it be one's own body or another's or, more accurately, the way bodies interact and face the risk of child-bearing and its threats. There is always and necessarily ignorance about motive, about reaction, about health, about resources, about the future, about the possibility of life itself. Thus marriages are ordered so as to be sustained or even stumble along in the midst of such ignorance. Marriages, as I have indicated, are "political" entities in the broad sense in that they are negotiated, rebelled against and within, are borne with, are suffered, are (one hopes) redeemed, all within a realm of ordered and disordered human interaction. True love—if we are to speak in such abstract terms—or the love of the nuptial mystery, whatever it in fact ends up being, must at root be a love that gives itself into the midst of such an ignorance, and therefore into the history of imperfect ordering. If there *is* an intrinsic connection or at least analogy (using the term loosely) between the love of the nuptial mystery and God's own self, it must include this center of love as given in and into the midst of ignorance. The demand of "difference"—the other person, the other sex, the other time, the other sets of pressures and contingencies that cascade upon a life together—is self-giving *into* ignorance, not into some certain knowledge. Why people get married to this or that person is very hard to say or define, certainly in a way that can make sense of plural cases taken as a whole. We know that, historically, the shape of marriage's arrangement and ordering has varied significantly even in the Christian Church. But one thing that is fair to say is that twenty-first century Western versions of what this ordering of marriage "should" be have no privilege, in the claims to freedom or knowledge, over earlier or non-Western types. Either way, do we really know about each other, about ourselves, about the future and what it will bring?

One reason why the claim to forge some logical link between the life of God's own self and marriage is probably *im*proper, is because it effectively does away with this reality of love arising and working itself out within historical ignorance. This is true whether we wish to look at marriage from the perspective of creation in general, or within the "order of redemption" as theologians say. God's creation of life *is*, at its root, God's own creation of that which is ignorant of almost all things including itself. So God's creation of life involves also, somehow, God own willingness, therefore, to "live" with ignorance. I am not sure what this means, exactly, given the assertion we *must* properly make regarding God's omniscience. But it certainly means, in the order of redemption, that God's own self-giving into created human flesh (how impossible this is to comprehend!) is indeed, as Gore insisted with his "kenotic" framing of the Incarnation, a giving over into the demands of ignorance. If we are going to speak of God's own "life as Trinity" for himself (what theologians call the "immanent Trinity") we must say that the line between Trinity and Incarnation is ontologically unbridgeable: there is *no* logical coherence between the life of God and a life apart from God. Yet who can deny that just such a coherence has, in God's own act, come to be? Hence the Incarnation has about it a miraculous *ex nihilo* status. The Incarnation takes place precisely because God the life-giver, the inventor of ignorance itself because He is the inventor of history, becomes a life-bearing body. God has made marriage "from nothing" because marriage's form and history are grounded in the incomprehensible invention of life-bearing bodies. Marriage exists, within this strange and finite world that is ours, as an *analogia creationis*, an analogy of creation from the hand of God, not to himself, not between Father and Son and Spirit, not as desire or delight or who knows what, but from the wrenching of being into a strange realm of freedom, where only the giving away for all things gives life. That is to say, we cannot read human marriage off from the Trinity; we can read it off, theologically, only from the cross.[33]

This is where, I believe, so much modern effort to ground the mystery of human marriage in something "other than itself," other than the givenness of bodies in their life-bearing vocation, is wrongly founded. A recent overview of modern Roman Catholic theology by the British Dominican Fergus Kerr is subtitled, "From Neoscholasticism to Nuptial Mysticism." Kerr, interestingly, sees one of the key developments of twentieth-century Catholic theology to be the reorientation of theology as a whole towards this category or reality known as "the nuptial mystery."[34] Behind this development lie the works of people like Barth and von Balthasar, and, of course, the careful and stark articulations of John Paul II and even, to a lesser extent, the current Pope. It is a development Kerr is not altogether happy about, calling it "baffling" and out of step with "classical" Catholic tradition, precisely in the place where it deduces human sexuality from some inner-trinitarian reality. Did not Augustine himself quite explicitly *rule out* a trinitarian analogy that was

---

33. My point here is meant to oppose the notion that the cross itself can be somehow "overcome" within the life of God, because it is somehow a part of God's own inner Trinitarian self-engagement. Ironically, this notion, designed to take seriously the reality of evil in the world, has often tended to provide for a means of obscuring its inevitably informative role in the world's structures: if a part of the world because it is a part of God's life first, the cross' "divine overcoming" is also intrinsic to human history somehow, and therefore can, at least logically, be overleapt when defining the "true" structures that ought to shape human life. This ends up, often, in approaching the moral responsibilities of human life in terms of what "lies behind" our particularities—in the case of marriage certainly not procreative struggle, since this is only a "moment" in the divine life that is itself overcome and, hence, cannot ever be "normative" in their particularities. Jurgen Moltmann is probably most associated with this approach, as well as exemplary of its ironic character. Cf. the moving chapter 2 of his *The Trinity and the Kingdom: The Doctrine of God* (London: SCM, 1981) 21–60. But the cross is never "overcome" within human history. It is the only divine "overcoming" to which we can point or which we can articulate. A broad attempt to hold together aspects of both the communitarian analogies of the Trinity with the Christological concreteness of the cross—unsuccessfully, in my mind, but very precisely located in the meaning of human marriage—is Earl C. Muller's *Trinity and Marriage in Paul: The Establishment of a Communitarian Analogy of the Trinity Grounded in the Theological Shape of Pauline Thought* (New York: Peter Lang, 1990).

34 Fergus Kerr, *Twentieth-Century Catholic Theologians: From Neoscholasticism to Nuptial Mysticism* (Oxford: Blackwell, 2007) 81–83; 135–44; 175–79; 193–201; 214–21.

nuptially figured?[35] Yet, as Kerr points out, it was Cardinal Ratzinger who oversaw the claim that "the nuptial meaning of the body finds its realization in the human intimacy and love that mirror the communion of the Blessed Trinity."[36] While this is often linked to procreation by people like John Paul II, and to male–female difference, it need not be. More to the point, as Kerr intimates, it makes the Trinity a *mandate* for sexual behavior or sexual relations—behavior that, as we all well know, can be embraced in a number of directions whose diverse cultural shapes are filled with moral shadows.

The "image of God" that is the human being's created character is, to be sure, not simply explained by reference to a "way of being" or to some general set of dispositions, and we can be grateful to both Barth and John Paul II for insisting that physical form is not irrelevant to the *imago*.[37] But the matter of sexual difference cannot apply to the *imago* in any reductive manner. Certainly, no one would wish to imply that there is some logical connection between John Paul II and proponents of gay marriage. But once a "nuptial hermeneutics" becomes central to the understanding of divine life, rather than describing the straightforward historical reality of different bodies ordered to procreation, all kinds of strange things become possible theologically—Trinity as a family, primordial androgyns,[38] high-flying energies of *eros* and *agape*, dismissals of procreation altogether as being central to human vocation—that, despite one's best intentions, cannot logically avoid allowing the concrete

---

35. Kerr does not himself point this out; but see Augustine *De Trinitate* 12.3.3—6.8. And he does this because of the intrinsically *corporeal* character of nuptiality.

36. Cited in Kerr, *Twentieth-Century Catholic Theologians*, 197.

37. And Barth is not the only one. See among Roman Catholics Dom Charles Massabki's massive and unjustly overlooked synthesis *Le Christ: rencontre de deux amours* (Paris: Éditions de la Source, 1958) 105, 106–42, 1220–88, and Pierre Grelot, *Le Couple Humain dans l'Écriture* (Paris: Éditions du Cerf, 1962) 85–105. The notion, e.g., in Massabki, that the Trinity is a kind of "fecund" family wherein the Holy Spirit is the fruit of a union between Father and Son, is scripturally barren, despite its ongoing attraction. But it also is an example of the oddities associated with speculations regarding the "immanent" Trinity.

38 The line between the trajectories of these kinds of speculations and reductive Gnostic marginalizations of classical Christian claims can be seen in, e.g., the way that a modern rabbinic apologist for Jewish neutralization of Christian particularity, Elijah Benamozegh, dismisses Christian Trinitarianism precisely as a symbol of "family" androgynic relations similar to other religious attitudes implanted deeply in the human psyche. See his *Israel and Humanity* (Mahwah, NJ: Paulist, 1995) 271–72. The *Gospel of Philip* (118) provides testimony to the ancient Gnostic myths surrounding these kinds of speculations.

mediatorial role of Jesus to waver altogether.[39] Because bodies have to do with their historical role as life-bearers (this is bound simply to their status as creatures, in a world of time, where life is what it is *because* it orders itself to propagate itself) we cannot *today* extricate our discussions of marriage from the reality of human sin, the corruption of bodies and relations, and the final historical demand of Christ's own incarnation, his words, teaching, life, passion, death, and resurrection. These become the limits. Nothing representative or correspondent (to use terms often applied to analogical reasoning) lies "behind" them, no communal trinities or divine desires or internal diversities. Only a life created, assaulted, protected, restored, and passed on.

An unbeliever like the American poet Carl Sandburg might well remind today's Christians of the more obvious reality that theological speculation has obscured in its attempts to capture God's ahistorical form for historical purposes. The banal title of one of his poems, however, is just such a reminder:

> Being Born Is Important
>
> You who have stood at the bedposts and seen a mother on
> her high harvest day,
> the day of the most golden of harvest moons for her.
>
> You who have seen the new wet child dried behind the ears,
> swaddled in soft fresh garments,
> pursing its lips and sending a groping mouth toward
> nipples where white milk
> is ready
>
> You who have seen this love's payday
> of wild toiling and sweet agonizing—[40]
> You know being born is important.
> You know that nothing was ever so important to you
> You understand that the payday of love is so old,
> so involved, so traced with circles of the moon,

---

39. Cf. Douglas Farrow's trenchant critique of Eugene Rogers on this score, in "Beyond Nature, Shy of Grace," *International Journal of Systematic Theology* 5 (2003) 279. It is not logically irrelevant that the West's most ardent (and prolific) philosopher of "desire," Michel Onfray, is also its most single-minded anti-Christian (and monotheistic) thinker. Contemporary theologians have simply not examined with care the logical entailments to placing "desire" at the center of a discussion of God's nature and creation's character in relation to it.

40. This is, in part, what Steinberg says we must see when we look at Jesus' sexualized birth.

> so cunning with the secrets of the salts of the blood
> It must be older than the moon, older than salt.

"Older," yes, but therefore, by definition, lodged in time. It is here that we search for the truth of the nuptial mystery. I was ordained a priest in Burundi, Africa, where I had gone as a young deacon to serve the Anglican church there. In the village church where the bishop, Samuel Sindamuka, ordained me, there were gathered hundreds of people, sitting on the floor or standing in the back in the dust, wrapped in their colorful, or simply ragged cloaks. They were women, widows, orphans, able-bodied and ill. My Kirundi wasn't good, but the gist of Bishop Sindamuka's sermon was this: God chose the Jews in Palestine thousands of years ago. He nurtured them, and protected their lives and their children, in all the kinds of troubles and sorrows that people have, just like here in Burundi (Oh my! And how like the Book of Kings in its outcome among us!). And out of this somehow surviving people, he brought forth a body, *His* body, Jesus's body, to wrestle back his creation from simple disappearance and death. And then, this Jewish God with a body, risen from the dead, sent out his apostles, and year by year they and their disciples and their churches pressed forward, bearing the news and means of this redeemed life, passing it on from generation to generation, until at last, through so many births and deaths, it came south, across deserts and mountains, after centuries, even to Burundi, to us. "And look!" he said, pointing at me. He insisted on thinking I was Jewish, even though I had long explained to him that my mother was a Gentile. "Look!" he said, triumphantly. "Here is a Jew! Come among the Barundi, now in one body with them in Christ! The mission of Abraham is proved! Thanks be to God!" Then he turned to me and said, not tritely, but as one in the face of a deep mystery, "And please, Efrayimu, thank your mother and your father for us as well!" I think this has got the order right, theologically and historically, properly identified and celebrated.

6

Visions of Marriage in Ephesians 5

Roy R. Jeal

The task here, as it is in the earlier essay on Romans 1, is to examine and interpret the foundational biblical material that informs our topic: "the nuptial mystery." Here once again, the obvious first step is to determine where to look in the Bible in order to have productive discussion.[1] When it comes to marriage and "the nuptial mystery" the central New Testament passage is Eph 5:22–33, where the "mystery," of marriage is explicit: "This is a great *mystery*, and I speak of Christ and of the church" (5:32). Yet to read, interpret, and understand this text is highly problematic from the outset on several levels. The exegetical, theological, and socio-cultural issues inherent in and raised by the passage make it not only difficult—perhaps among the most interpretively puzzling passages in the entire New Testament[2]—but they make it a flash point for emotion and debate. It raises practical issues that have generated and frequently continue to generate sharp emotional reactions because of what it says and because of how it has been employed in and out of the Church. Many people consider some of its directives about women/wives to be unjust.[3]

---

1. See the comments in chapter 2 in this volume, "Ideology, Argumentation and Social Direction in Romans 1."

2. Certainly more complex and difficult exegetically, theologically, and ethically than Romans 1, the focus of my earlier article in this volume.

3. See the discussion in Charles H. Talbert, *Ephesians and Colossians* (Grand Rapids: Baker, 2007) 149–53.

Some readers think that some things the passage says are simply wrong.[4] Standing over these practical concerns are important grammatical and argumentation issues regarding where the flow of ideas begins and how they progress,[5] and the much-debated questions about the sources and the intertextual connections of the entire domestic code (5:22—6:9).[6]

When Eph 5:22-33 is read, when it speaks aloud,[7] it places images of women, men, their bodies, and marriage in readers' minds. It also evokes *pictures* of Christ and the *ekklēsia*, both envisioned as bodies. This effect, which can be termed *phanopoeia*, or "rhetography,"[8] occurs naturally when people read texts. When people read (or listen to) literature of all kinds—novels, dramas, short stories, poetry, non-fiction, biographies, letters, technical materials—they are drawn into the visuality of the texts. They "see" scenes and visualize persons, places, and things, they "hear" sounds, notice colors, they visualize and hear and feel the emotions. These visual things not only contribute, but tend to dominate their understanding of the text and the information (meaning) it conveys. All of us can recognize this. The visual scenes cast in the imagination can dramatically affect people emotionally. The Bible, broadly speaking, is a rhetorical narrative that presents images of people, places, actions, things, and ideas with which audiences of readers and hearers must grapple and engage, which they must mentally frame and contextualize, which they must mentally *visualize* in order to be drawn into the worlds being portrayed and the modes of discourse being employed, and be led along to reshaped, restructured lives lived in God's kingdom. Considering the visioning intentionally brings into sight the situations that the biblical texts want their audiences to grasp and play out in their own lives. The visual imagery aims to *do* things to people, to evoke a disposition of

---

4. Not to mention the directives about slaves and their masters in Eph 6:5-9.

5. Does the direct context and grammatical structure begin with and necessarily connect with 5:18-21, or is 5:22—6:9 to be interpreted as a freestanding unit?

6. Does the domestic code come from Jewish or Hellenistic materials or is it a Christian or Pauline formulation? Intertextuality with traditional topical discussions of households in ancient literature seems clear. On this see the commentaries.

7. The NT documents have distinct oral/aural and rhetorical qualities. They were read aloud to their first audiences, the vast majority of whom were illiterate.

8. On this, see Vernon K. Robbins, "Rhetography: A New Way of Seeing the Familiar Text," in *Words Well Spoken: George Kennedy's Rhetoric of the New Testament*, ed. C. C. Black and D. F. Watson (Waco: Baylor University Press, 2008) 81-106; Roy R. Jeal, "Blending Two Arts: Rhetorical Words, Rhetorical Pictures and Social Formation in the Letter to Philemon," *Sino-Christian Studies* 5 (2008) 9-38.

mind, to shape readers' and listeners' responses and understandings to the ideas being presented. Consequently, understanding something of the visual rhetoric of Ephesians 5 will help us understand the point and the effect of the passage.

VISIONS AND VISUALITY

Ephesians 5:22–33 has an ecclesiological view and context. It envisions the Church as an embodied entity, as the body of Christ. It is very important to grasp this, particularly because the context is often (mis-) understood as a straightforward paraenetical directive comprised of paradigmatic rules to be followed and virtues to be performed, and, frankly, as a divine description of a Christian family hierarchy and as male–female heterosexism.[9] What readers are to *see* there, however, is not just instructions about marriage, but the Church (the *ekklēsia*/ assembly) as the body (*sōma*) of Christ. The Church as the chosen, adopted, redeemed people of God, has been in view since the beginning of Ephesians (cf. 1:3–7), explicitly so as the body of Christ since 1:22–23 (cf. 2:16; 3:6; 4:4, 12, 16). The Church is visibly in motion, engaging in its proper role of worship (3:20–21), "walking worthily" of the calling of the gospel (4:1),[10] in its understanding of the "mystery" of God that has been made known to it (cf. 3:9).[11] The point is that the Church is here visible in its own ecclesiological space, and is being encouraged to keep moving along in this space, with the assistance of its gifted people (among whom are apostles, prophets, evangelists, pastors, teachers, 4:7–11), toward maturity of the body (4:12–16). The behaviors of wives and husbands as married persons are seen in this space, within the body/church as part of it and in relationship to it. There is a visible setting where the *ekklēsia* and the players in it are engaging in their respective roles.

The actions are observably part of worship activities in the assembly. This becomes clear when the thoughts that begin at 5:18 are taken

---

9. Cf. Elisabeth Schüssler Fiorenza, *In Memory of Her: A Feminist Theological Reconstruction of Christian Origins*. (New York: Crossroad, 1984) especially 266–70; Cynthia Briggs Kittredge, *Community and Authority: The Rhetoric of Obedience in the Pauline Tradition* (Harrisburg: Trinity, 1998).

10. Walking (*peripatein*) as a metaphor for moving along through life, is the explicit imagery employed. Note that some English Bibles such as the New Revised Standard Version do not use the term.

11. Particularly as a Gentile church (or church*es* on the view that Ephesians is a circular letter).

into account.[12] A clear step in the progression of ideas and scenes occurs here where the Church is visualized taking on the wise behavior of being filled with the Spirit. Intoxification is refused and filling with God's Spirit is welcomed into the bodies and thinking of the people in the assembly. This filling is characterized in the visual scene by five worship actions indicated by five participial statements:[13] "speaking [singing] to each other [yourselves]" (*lalountes heautois*); "singing and singing praises[14] in your hearts" (*adontes kai psallontes tē kardia humōn*); "giving thanks at all times for all things" (*eucharistountes pantote huper pantōn*); and "submitting to each other" (*hypotassomenoi allēlois*). These worship actions are practiced together, that is, in the church/assembly. Each of these "Spirit-filled" actions is a physical body action and the visualization of them makes it clear that each action is practiced for the sake of other persons, not for self-benefit. This is a crucially important thing to see. The concern of the portrayal is not about the growth and maturation of individuals who speak, sing, offer thanks and submit themselves. The scene, rather, anticipates benefits that accrue to the growth of the church community and that glorify God. This image is instructive for understanding the mystery of the gospel and the mystery of marriage.

While the following section presents imperatives to wives, husbands, children, parents, slaves, and masters, and is usually called a domestic or household code (*haustafel*; 5:22—6:9), it cannot be separated from the picturing of the active church/body of Christ that has been in view in Ephesians for some time. The portrayal does not abruptly shift to the domestic and private situations in readers' homes apart from life in the community of believers, despite the tendency of interpreters to describe it as a discrete passage. The players are part of the church community and the behaviors they are called to practice and which we visualize them actually doing *mentally and bodily* in the visualization are done in the ecclesiological space and are another step in the action. The domestic code is employed as a *topos* (i.e., a topic or commonplace) to convey understanding of the points being made regarding the behavior of people in the believing community. Wives are called directly by Paul's

---

12. The sentence (in Greek) may be understood to begin at 5:18 or even at 5:15.

13. The participles are dependent on the imperative verb *plērousthe* in 5:18 and describe what it means to be filled with the Spirit, that is, they describe what it looks like to be committed to the Spirit's leading. Those committed to the Holy Spirit do these things.

14. "Singing praises" is often given as "making melody" or similar phrase in order to smooth out the diction.

voice[15] (vocative *hai gynaikes*) to submit to their own husbands and we imagine them doing it.[16] They are doing this in the same way that they submit themselves to the Lord (i.e., Jesus). They are not being forced into subjection either bodily or mentally, but do so according to instruction. The argument for what is being observed is given in 5:23–24:

> *Case*: wives submit to their husbands.
>
> *Rationale*: "because the husband is the head of the wife just as Christ is the head of the church, himself saviour of the body."
>
> *Result*: (the understanding that) ". . . as the church is subject to Christ, so also wives are to their husbands in everything."

There is a visible male–female hierarchy here that reflects the Mediterranean domestic conventions of the time where the household and the family typically operated under the authority of the *paterfamilias*.[17] But let us see the picture as it is fully presented before stating views or drawing conclusions about the hierarchy or about social conventions.[18] The hierarchy is not authoritarian or oppressive. We can hear husbands being directly addressed by Paul's voice to "love the wives" (where the imperative "love," *agapate*, indicates not romantic or emotional love, but an intentional, decided love), and we observe the believing husbands doing it in physical action and in mental determination. The husbands are giving themselves over completely for their wives just like Christ gave himself over completely for the sake of the Church. The argumentative rationale for this behavior is seen in the action described in 5:26–30:

> *Case*: husbands love their wives.
>
> *Rationale*: because they are to behave like Christ who gave himself up for the church. Since Christ did this in order to present the Church to himself as a holy and unblemished wife,[19] husbands

---

15. Of course the questions about the authorship of Ephesians are recognized, but the implied voice claims to be Paul's.

16. There is no verb in the Greek of 5:22. The statement relies clearly on the participle hypotassomenoi in 5:21.

17. For a good general discussion, see David A. deSilva, *Honor, Patronage, Kinship and Purity: Unlocking New Testament Culture* (Downers Grove, IL: InterVarsity, 2000) 158–97, particularly 178–93.

18. There is every reason to think that ancient Mediterranean people would not initially be shocked or annoyed by the instruction, since the hierarchy would seem socially ordinary.

19. While the Church is not explicitly called the wife of Christ, the inference is clear and unmistakeable. Cf. Rev 19:7; 21:2, 9; 22:17.

are portrayed giving themselves up so that their wives are seen to be holy and unblemished wives/women. In a second argumentative step (houtōs, in the same way), husbands are obligated (opheilousin) to love their wives because they know that they honour and care for their *own* bodies just as Christ honors and cares for *his* body, the Church. No one in the scene portrayed ever hates his own flesh.[20] Christ himself actually cares for the flesh in the form of the ekklēsia. Christ cares in this manner because (he knows that) "we" (i.e., we the church) are parts of his own body.

Result: wives and the Church are clearly portrayed as *glorious* (5:27) bodies.

The rhetoric is powerful, graphic, and compelling. Husbands are showing their wives as thoroughly pure and beautiful. Though the author knows that the Church does have its issues and that wives are likely to have blemishes, the realities of present existence are irrelevant. The husbands are completely dedicated to showing that their wives are beautiful. The purpose of the self-giving love is to make the wife, that is, the Church, the body, glorious. With this imagery the nuptial mystery begins to come more fully into view and to take centre stage in the portrayal.

One thing that becomes clear in the visualization is that when the wives are submitting themselves to their husbands they are not being oppressed, without independence, or otherwise mistreated, however patriarchal the scene may appear to be.[21] They are given dignity and glory regardless of their flaws. They go through "cleansing in the bath of water in word" (5:26).[22] They are "nourished" and "cherished" (5:29). The dignity and glory comes to them not by means of a superiority or inherent dignity and glory found in the husbands, but because the husbands give themselves over completely—in the imagery over to death, just like

---

20. Here "flesh" (sarx) is used, a change from "body" (*sōma*) emphasizing the distinctly physical nature of the visual bodies that are envisioned. This vocabulary change also emphasizes the "flesh," that is, the particularly human aspect of existence that tends toward sin, that requires the cleansing suggested in 5:26-27 and the care indicated in 5:29. Husbands love their own flesh and the flesh of their wives, just as Christ loves the flesh which is the church.

21. Of course, I say this as a man and so, unavoidably, from a gendered position.

22. Perhaps a visual allusion to the ritual bath of a bride before her wedding. Ezek 16:8-14 envisions how God provided such a bath for the (female) Israel (Talbert, *Ephesians and Colossians*, 142).

Christ—for their sake. The hierarchy is not focused on domination, but on determined good for the wife.[23]

The church/body/marriage depiction of husbands and wives plays out in the nuptial or matrimonial mystery portrayed still more graphically in 5:31–33:

> "For this reason a man will leave his father and mother and be joined to his wife, and the two will become one flesh." This is a great mystery, and I am applying it to Christ and the church. Each of you, however, should love his wife as himself, and a wife should respect her husband.

Now as we watch the husbands and wives during the process of becoming married,[24] a man moves away from his own parents, from the space in which he was bodily conceived and nurtured and in which he matured, and he moves toward another space where stands the woman who is his wife and there he is joined to her, the two becoming one flesh in sexual intercourse.[25] This is described as "the great mystery" (*to mystērion touto mega estin*, 5:32). It draws obviously on the story of the man and the woman created by God according to Gen 2:24, which Ephesians employs as a confirmation for what husbands and wives do. The matrimonial mystery involves movement away from the life one has known in a particular space with all of its implications, and into a life in a different yet specified space with its own implications. The implications of the new space are explicated, i.e., what was hidden is revealed, where the husband has given himself over for the glory of the wife. The wife and husband become body and flesh (*sōma* and *sarx*) of each other; the two become a unit, a single flesh, a bonded entity.

The glorious body in the visualized mystery is the female body, whether the wife or the *ekklēsia*,[26] and the glorious body is presented

---

23. Hierarchies are not necessarily oppressive. Certainly they often become oppressive. The Anglican episcopal hierarchy, for example, is not meant to be oppressive, but seeks the good of the Church and the glory of God.

24. A flashback in the visualization. The Greek verbs are futures as in LXX Gen 2:24, but the scene is still visualized at the earlier time in the husbands' and wives' lives.

25. For Paul it is sexual intercourse that enacts the bond, that is the actual physical uniting that is "one flesh." He makes this clear in 1 Cor 6:12–20. There is, interestingly, significant research indicating that sexual intercourse brings about emotional and even chemical bonding between persons. This (partially) accounts for the "emotional ties" that people experience after having sex several times.

26. *Ekklēsia* (*hē ekklēsia*) is a feminine noun in Greek.

as such by the husband and by Christ who are analogous to each other. They (the husbands and Christ) function as "head" not in the authoritarian sense but as "source," i.e., as providers of glory. The author states emphatically[27] that he speaks about Christ and the Church (5:32). Wise church and body behavior, which remains central to the context, is characterized by the picture of the matrimonial mystery. That is, it is where, as we noticed in the imagery of 5:18–21, the actions and determined affections are directed not toward self and self-benefit, but toward others and their benefit. This is at the heart of the mystery: it is about how actions like submission and love are directed toward the glorious presentation of others. Underlying this are the hidden realities that are now revealed (for that is what the word "mystery" implies) in what God in Christ has done for humans. It is, in other words, about what Christ has done for the Church by giving himself for it (5:29) as it is similarly about what the husband does (and how he does it), i.e., he loves his wife. Husbands do not get away without submitting. Indeed they submit wholly, giving up everything, life itself, for the sake and the purpose of the others, their glorious wives. So, in the visualization, husbands are loving their wives as themselves and the wives are respecting their husbands (5:33).

But the vision of the mystery runs deeper than this in Ephesians 5. To see it we must look at some other things in the letter. The nuptial space is not only different, it is transcendent. The mystery of marriage and of the Church draws on the creational narrative of Gen 2:24 and anticipates the restoration and reunification of both, and in fact the restoration and reunification of "all things" to the creational and heavenly mode. Indeed the images of marriage and Church as they are portrayed show us wives and husbands actually playing out the anticipated creational-eschatological realities in the physical bodies of real persons already in the present time. So the passage is not more concerned about one relationship—wives and husbands or Christ and Church—than the other. Believers participate directly in the "mystery" by living lives of heaven (frequently in Ephesians stated as "the heavenlies" or "heavenly places," 1:3, 20; 2:6; 3:10; 6:12) in the *ekklēsia*. This has been in mind from the beginning of Ephesians where it is claimed that God

> ... has made known to us the *mystery* of his will, according to his good pleasure that he purposed in him, with a view toward

---

27. Indicated in Greek by the first person pronoun ("I") plus the first person singular verb.

the economy of the fullness of the times, to sum up all things in Christ, things in the heavens and things on the earth. (1:9–10)[28]

The mystery that has been made known is the mystery of God's will that had a view toward the fullness of the times when all things, that is, the entire cosmos of things in the heavens and things on the earth, will be brought to a sum in Christ. Christ himself is the center of God's mystery which has a clear trajectory in the progression of ideas to a particular action and place: the space where Christ and God are praised in their glory (to the praise of his glory, 1:12, 14).[29] This revealed mystery is something the author of Ephesians wants audiences of the letter to understand. The author prays that people will know what a great and marvelous thing God has done in Christ's resurrection, to which glorious thing God calls them:

> I pray that the God of our Lord Jesus Christ, the Father of glory, may give you a spirit of wisdom and revelation in knowledge of him, so that, with the eyes of your heart enlightened, you may know what is the hope to which he has called you, what are the riches of his glorious inheritance among the saints, and what is the immeasurable greatness of his power for us who believe, according to the working of his great power which he worked in Christ, raising him from the dead and seating him at his right hand in the heavenly places, far above all rule and authority and power and dominion, and above every name that is named, not only in this age but also in the coming age. And he put all things under his feet and gave him as head over all things for (the benefit of) the church, which is his body, the fullness of him who fills everything full. (1:17–23)

This is the revealed mystery: God has in Christ performed an apocalyptic act for the benefit of the others, for the *ekklēsia*. Christ has been raised and continues to sit in power at God's right hand for the benefit of the Church. Christ gave and continues to give himself over for the sake of the Church, just as husbands are to give themselves over for the sake of their wives. As the prayer suggests, it takes eyes of hearts that have been enlightened to see this. It takes the capturing of a vision, of the visions of marriage.

---

28. My translation.

29. For more detail on this, see Roy R. Jeal, "An Unusual Christology: The Exalted Christ in Ephesians," in *Currents in Biblical and Theological Dialogue*, ed. J. K. Stafford (Winnipeg: St. John's, 2002) 69–88, 72–78.

The mystery is clarified more fully in Eph 3:2–12:

> surely you have already heard of the commission of God's grace that was given me for you, and how the *mystery* was made known to me by revelation, as I wrote above in a few words, a reading of which will enable you to perceive my understanding of the *mystery* of Christ. In former generations this *mystery* was not made known to humankind, as it has now been revealed to his holy apostles and prophets by the Spirit: that is, the Gentiles have become fellow heirs, members of the same body, and sharers in the promise in Christ Jesus through the gospel. Of this gospel I have become a servant according to the gift of God's grace that was given me by the working of his power. Although I am the very least of all the saints, this grace was given to me to bring to the Gentiles the news of the boundless riches of Christ, and to make everyone see what is the plan of the *mystery* hidden for ages in God who created all things; so that through the church the wisdom of God in its rich variety might now be made known to the rulers and authorities in the heavenly places. This was in accordance with the eternal purpose that he has carried out in Christ Jesus our Lord, in whom we have access to God in boldness and confidence through faith in him.

The mystery is about God's actions in Christ that have brought about the inclusion, in other words the unity and equality, of Gentiles and Jews in the one body, the *ekklēsia*. All are "sharers" in the promise of Christ in the gospel and approach God boldly and confidently through faith.[30] This, Paul is visualized saying, was God's hidden plan, God's eternal purpose, that is now revealed. This inclusion, unity, and equality is seen very clearly in the scene described in Eph 2:11–22:

> So then, remember that at one time you Gentiles by birth, called "the uncircumcision" by those who are called "the circumcision"— a physical circumcision made in the flesh by human hands— remember that you were at that time without Christ, being aliens from the commonwealth of Israel, and strangers to the covenants of promise, having no hope and without God in the world. But now in Christ Jesus *you who once were far off have been brought near by the blood of Christ.* For he is our peace; in his flesh he has made both groups into one and has broken down the dividing wall, that is, the hostility between us. He has abolished the law

---

30. Literally through Christ's own faith, *dia tēs pisteōs autou*, read as a subjective genitive.

> with its commandments and ordinances, *that he might create in himself one new humanity* in place of the two, thus making peace, *and might reconcile both groups to God in one body through the cross*, thus putting to death that hostility through it. So he came and proclaimed peace to you who were far off and peace to those who were near; for through him both of us have access in one Spirit to the Father. So then you are no longer strangers and aliens, but you are citizens with the saints and also members of the household of God, built upon the foundation of the apostles and prophets, with Christ Jesus himself as the cornerstone. In him the whole structure is joined together and grows into a holy temple in the Lord; in whom you also are built together into a dwelling place for God in the Spirit.

Marriage is to be understood in light of the grand cosmic drama that is presented visually in Ephesians. Disparate groups of people are brought together, live together in peace, and function as God's dwelling. The space of this existence is the "heavenly places" (the heavenlies, 2:6; 3:10), where, in a proleptic way, believers are sitting with Christ and living out the heavenly life. The Church plays out the creational-eschatological mode in its own body life and in the actual physical bodies of people. This is the drama of salvation and the space where everything has been done for the benefit of the saved, the Church. The nuptial mystery is one piece of it and one perspective on it. Wives and husbands order their bodily lives in accord with what Christ has done for the Church so that the Church will be what it is, a glorious, apocalyptically shaped body. In this apocalyptic space the creational scene of Gen 2:24 is lived out in anticipation of the eschatological completeness of all things being summed up in Christ.

VISUAL IMPLICATIONS

Ephesians 5 provides a fairly wide-ranging visualization of church-body and human-body activities along with rationales for practicing them. The visualization creates a kind of moving picture for the Church and for Christian faith and behavior, a trajectory in which believers place themselves and according to which they shape their lives. It is not difficult now for us to see the leading visual implications for formation that are set out in the passage.

The vision for marriage in Ephesians 5 is a gospel and body visioning. It reflects and participates in what God has done for the salvation of humans by his gracious activity in Christ (cf. 2:8). What Christ did was nothing less than to present the Church as the glorious image of the fulfillment of the ages. Fundamental to this is that God and Christ have acted and continue to act not for self-benefit but for the benefit of the Church. This is very much at the heart of the *mystery* of the gospel and of the *mystery* of marriage and of the *mystery* of becoming one flesh. In Ephesians (and in the NT)[31] the direction of thought, action, and relationship is aimed toward the Church and toward wives and husbands, and never toward self-benefit or self-indulgence. The nuptial mystery is that marriage is for the good of the other person. Marriage in this picture is not concerned with individual and personal needs, proclivities or desires, and certainly not with personal fulfillment and acquisitions. This is a different way than how things typically operated in the ancient Mediterranean authoritarian social convention where the *paterfamilias* was the authoritarian, kyriarchal figure who dominated the family (which included not only immediate relatives but all who lived in the household, including slaves) for the sake of maintaining honor in the community.[32] Ephesians 5 actually envisions a non-authoritarian wife–husband relationship where each behaves with the other in mind. They come together to form a single unit, one flesh, where each seeks the good (indeed the pleasure?) of the other, the wife/female of the husband/male and the husband/male of the wife/female. The mystery of Christ giving himself up for the Church is the underlying imagery for this and, certainly in the view of Ephesians, the underlying reality for it. Christ and the Church continue to play out these roles for each other and Christian wives and husbands are encouraged to live them out, too. The trajectory is heavenly. It anticipates the eternal life promised in and brought about by the gospel, living it already in the present, in the presence of evil and in resistance to it. This is an envisioning of the Church. Eph subverts the usual hierarchical social structure of the time by showing Christ's submission to the Church. If an imperial analogy could be conceived, it would be the imagery of the emperor giving his life up for the sake of the empire. Equality and dignity are not here gained by force,

---

31. See, for example, Gal 5:13—6:10, where freedom is described as an opportunity to become slaves of others, not as an opportunity for the flesh (self-indulgence).

32. See deSilva, *Honor, Patronage*, 178–93.

128   *The Nuptial Mystery*

by rights, or by self-determination. They are gained as the blessings of God and are then enacted by believers. This is the mystery: God blesses the Church with fullness and salvation and dignity for all in it. Ephesians 5 calls for believers to grasp and physically embody this mystery, particularly in marriage.

Images arouse expectancy. There is a rhetoric of expectancy that encourages audiences of Ephesians 5 to take on the roles and actions described.[33] Wives and husbands are literally called to their respective behaviors. The behavior of husbands in particular rhetoricizes an expectancy of a more than egalitarian situation for their wives; it is a privileged situation. Wives are not oppressed or suppressed, but glorified, elevated by husbands' love for them. Similarly, wives, by submitting themselves to their husbands do not thereby accept tyranny, they privilege their husbands. Ephesians does not explicitly reject hierarchy, but it does reject a gender-specific hierarchy where males dominate by force of power. The historically understood form of male–female hierarchy is deconstructed in the care of husbands for wives and in the submission of the wives. While the Greco-Roman approach in domestic codes was generally oppressive and restrictive,[34] Ephesians calls for submission to the spouse. Wives and husbands serve one another.

Another implication must be mentioned. The visual imagery (not to mention the Greek grammar) of Eph 5:22–33 portrays marriage as a heterosexual relationship. Christ is viewed as masculine and the Church as feminine, and husbands are distinctly males (indicated by *hoi andres*, 5:25; cf. 5:23, 24, 28) and wives are distinctly females (indicated by *hai gynaikes*, 5:22; cf. 5:23, 24, 25, 28, 33). There is no other vision of marriage here or elsewhere in Scripture. The image arouses the memory of how marriage has always been understood in biblical narrative, and it arouses the expectancy of what the marriages of believers are to look like. There is a male–female complementarity that is given its scriptural foundation in Genesis. Can people treat it otherwise? They can, of course, but when they do they move marriage outside of the heterosexual complementarity of Scripture and the narrative and rhetoric of Scripture to something that is not only not supported by Scripture but is considered by the Bible

---

33. There is no doubt also an opposing rhetoric of resistance against the exhortations, particularly when they are seen as heterosexist, patriarchal and kyriarchal.

34. Particularly, it may be noted, toward slaves, who were expected to be available for whatever sexual desires the master may have for them. See Robert Jewett, *Romans: A Commentary*, Hermeneia (Minneapolis: Fortress, 2007) 180–81.

to be unrighteous. Christians and the Church are called to live out their lives in obedience and righteousness. The Bible, by its own internal proclamation, and the *ekklēsia*, in its proclamation, liturgy, and traditions, call believers in Jesus Christ to obedience and righteousness. The Church is not called to approve what the Scripture itself opposes, it is called to glorify God, to proclaim the gospel, and to encourage faithfulness even in the face of stress, persecution, and death. The Church may be tolerant of whatever people do, indeed it might not always ask people what they do, but it may not approve behaviors that do not model the anticipated life of heaven already in the present and that stand against what is envisioned by scripture. Christians recognize that Christ died for all (cf. Rom 5:18–19; 2 Cor 5:14) and that the gospel is for all, yet they may not approve of what all believe or practice. The Church proclaims "times of refreshing" (Acts 3:20), not continuation of behaviors that do not align with scripture.

CONCLUSION

The mystery of marriage is the mystery of Christ. Jesus Christ gave himself up "even to death on a cross" (Phil 2:8) for the sake of the Church. He gave up his own body "in the likeness of sinful flesh" (Rom 8:3) in order to bind disparate groups together "in his flesh" (Eph 2:14). This saving work of Christ brings about the community called Church and it continues on for the benefit of the Church. The Church comes to fullness in Christ who is himself indwelt bodily by the fullness of God (Col 2:9–10). The members of the Church are members of the body of Christ and (are to) function together as a unit (1 Cor 12:12, 27). All the parts of the body—feet, ears, hands, eyes, as 1 Corinthians 12 eloquently points out—work with all the other parts for the good of the entire body. They are a unit, a single flesh, that honors and respects—that loves—the parts and the whole for the dignity and glory of the body. The Church is in its nature a caring community (cf. Acts 2:42–47). It is a community that sees to the needs of its people and of people outside of it. When it becomes self-centered and self-indulgent and when its members make it their aim to seize the day for themselves it stands in danger. This made very clear by Paul the Apostle:

> For you were called to freedom, brothers and sisters; only do not use your freedom as an opportunity for self-indulgence, but through love become slaves to one another. For the whole

> law is summed up in a single commandment, "You shall love your neighbor as yourself." If, however, you bite and devour one another, take care that you are not consumed by one another. (Gal 5:13-15)

As Christ gave himself for the Church so Christians are dedicated to the Church for the sake of all the others. Paul and many others have so lived their lives.

Marriage, according to Ephesians 5, properly operates in the same way. Wives and husbands live their lives not for their own sake or their own desires and surely not for their own pleasures but for the honor and glory of the other, wife for husband and husband for wife. The understanding of this is the deep nuptial mystery.

Sometimes a little knowledge gets in the way of understanding.[35] Sometimes knowledge of the questions about the sources or sociocultural, religious, and historical backgrounds of Ephesians 5 get in the way of seeing its connection with the marriage mystery. The vision of marriage that is presented, however, *shows us* how husbands and wives can live. Wise body and bodily behavior in marriage, where two disparate persons become one flesh, a unit, is the picture of the Church and of God's salvation in Christ. It anticipates the dignity and the goodness of the heavenly life, the blessed fullness of eternity.

Without any doubt, the *mystery* of our religion is great:

> He was revealed in flesh,
> vindicated in spirit,
> seen by angels,
> proclaimed among Gentiles,
> believed in throughout the world,
> taken up in glory. (1 Tim 3:16)

---

35. See Virginia Ramey Mollenkott, "Emancipative Elements in Ephesians 5.21–33: Why Feminist Scholarship Has (Often) Left Them Unmentioned and Why They Should Be Emphasized," in *A Feminist Companion to the Deutero-Pauline Epistles*, ed. Amy-Jill Levine (Cleveland: Pilgrim, 2003) 37–58.

7

Becoming One

The Christian Story and the Politics of Marriage

Christopher R. J. Holmes

I

Marriage has become a highly contested entity of late. Extremes on the right and the left in both political and ecclesiastical realms are treating it as a coveted good, a prize to be won. The outcome: marriage is something over which *we* preside and which we domesticate, all in accordance with our own aims and ambitions. As far as I am concerned, much of the debate currently taking place in the Anglican Church concerning matters of human sexuality and the nuptial mystery is rather stale, precisely because it proceeds according to a domesticated state of affairs. That is, it proceeds naturalistically, as if the redemptive work of the triune God were something of an afterthought. Hence my concern in this paper is to raise very basic theological questions, namely "What *is* marriage?" and "What is the *purpose* of marriage?" and to answer those questions in a way that yields to the ways and works of the God who has made all things new in Jesus Christ.

It is my contention that these two questions regarding marriage are not neutral questions. Neither individual Christians nor the eucharistic community of which they are members are transparent unto themselves, for the story by which they are narrated is a story that is given to them. That story is of course the story of the triune God as made known in the history of Israel and fulfilled in Jesus Christ. If such is the case, then marriage, as with the Christian and the Church, is not an entity that is to be understood in a closed fashion, impervious to the life-giving work of God in Christ. Indeed, marriage is not an entity that can be mapped *via* the world as we know it and understand it to be. The basic frame of reference for a decidedly Christian account of marriage, its being and its purpose, originates from and is bound to the reconciling activity of the triune God.

In this paper I will account for marriage in terms that are distinctly theological. In my judgment, there is one theological category that stands out in particular in the context of theological reflection on the nature and purpose of Christian marriage, and it is that of *covenant*. Covenant, says Karl Barth, is "the link which Yahweh has established between Himself and His people, which in His eternal faithfulness He has determined to keep, and which He for His part has continually renewed."[1] The covenant with Israel established by God and fulfilled by God in Jesus Christ is the starting and end point of an account of Christian marriage. Indeed, it is in relation to this covenant that the nature of marriage comes to the fore as a kind of "parable and sign" of God's steadfast covenantal love.[2] So, too, with marriage's purpose: it is an instrument of discipleship whereby a particular man and a particular woman are formed into people of the covenant.[3]

I will account for the nature and purpose marriage primarily in conversation with the Swiss Reformed theologian Karl Barth. I will also

---

1. Karl Barth, *Church Dogmatics*, Vol. III/1, *The Doctrine of Creation*, ed. T. F. Torrance and G. W. Bromiley (Edinburgh: T. & T. Clark, 1958) 315 [Hereafter *CD* III/1].

2. *CD* III/1, 315.

3. I emphasize the covenantal foundations of Christian marriage as a kind of corrective in relation to some "postliberal" treatments of marriage that cast marriage as a practice whose intelligibility arises first and foremost in relation to a polity, that is, the Church. Although I do not deny for a moment that the Church "as a polity of God's good news" is necessary in taking into account the nature and shape Christian marriage, I do take issue with the idea that the Church is somehow the *constitutive* context for an understanding of Christian marriage. Indeed, I rather think that marriage is intelligible only in relation to the active agency of God, and only then the Church, understood as the place where the active agent of the history of the covenant forms men and women into people of the covenant. For an example of an account that privileges the epistemic primacy of the Church, see David Matzko McCarthy, "Becoming One Flesh: Marriage, Remarriage, and Sex," in *The Blackwell Companion to Christian Ethics*, ed. Stanley Hauerwas and Samuel Wells (Malden, MA: Blackwell, 2004) 277.

engage, in the last section of the paper, in brief conversation with the recent and very sophisticated proposals of the British Anglican theologian Graham Ward. I think it wise to engage Ward because he offers a very lucid account of why it is fitting that the Christian community talk about marriage as *not* involving a particular man and a particular woman but rather two bodies of either the same sex or of different sexes. My aim in treating Ward is twofold. First, Ward shows us that there are salutary theological reasons for moving the discussion of marriage away from gender and toward bodies. Although I remained unconvinced in the end as to the fittingness of his particular moves, most especially his sense that sexual difference is not absolutely germane to anthropology, I believe that it is nonetheless important in an essay such as this to raise critical question in relation to what I would call a seriously *theological*, albeit nonetheless "revisionist," account.

II

When reflecting on the nature and purpose of marriage in the context of a church consultation, it is important to talk about God. Rather than marriage being an instrument of social or personal utility that meets our needs for intimacy, self-fulfillment, affection, etc., or being a way to self-actualization and a more authentic way of being human, I will argue that marriage is *not*, first and foremost, about us or about our needs. Quite the opposite: Christian marriage is about God, specifically, about witness to the triune God's saving works. Without the life-giving works of this God in mind, an account of Christian marriage and its ends will be subject to ideological whims and vagaries of one sort or another, and will proceed in a kind of vacuum, oblivious to the world-altering work of God in his gracious determination of humanity to be his covenant partners.

To talk about who God is, is, at the same time, to talk about what God does. According to the witness of the Old Testament, God elects a people for himself—Israel. Throughout the history of Israel, God keeps faith with a stubborn and recalcitrant people; it is a history that reads as a remarkably one-sided affair. Its one-sidedness is indicative of how the whole history of Israel points forward to the day when it will be fulfilled in Jesus Christ in "the co-existence of Christ and His community."[4] It is in Christ's marriage to the Church as conceived in the New Testament

---

4. *CD* III/1, 328

that marks the completion and culmination of Yahweh's covenantal purposes with Israel. Put again, Christ is the culmination of God's ways and works with sinful human beings, the ultimate manifestation of God's will to pardon and restore unfaithful and disobedient Jews and therewith Gentiles to life in covenantal communion. Accordingly, it is Jesus's life, death, and resurrection that is the center of all of God's redemptive activity. And it is imitation of Christ and of his self-giving in relation to the Church and to the world that is the key to understanding marriage's nature and purpose.

Moreover, the question of marriage raises the question of being human in general, that is, what it means to be a particular man or a particular woman created in the image and likeness of the triune God. Indeed, that the triune God establishes, maintains, and perfects covenantal communion with those whom he has created in his image, means just about everything for the self-understanding of a particular man and a particular woman, whether they be married or single. Specifically, it is the *union* that Christ Jesus has established between himself and the Christian community that is indeed the constitutive content for determining what it means to be human. To be human, says Barth, is to acknowledge that "this [covenantal] determination characterizes his [i.e., humanity's] being as being in encounter with his fellow-man."[5] If the human person is to understand herself aright, argues Barth, she must recognize herself as one who is created for communion as "a being in fellow-humanity."[6] Indeed, becoming human involves the living of a life of "freedom in fellowship with others," founded upon and sustained by the fellowship God has established with human beings in Christ Jesus.[7] Christopher Chenault Roberts expresses this well: "In and through their male and female differences, humans are commanded to be and do something no other animals do, which is to witness to God's own form of relational life."[8] But what does this life of witness and thus freedom look like, this life of freedom *for* and *in* communion with others and with God? What does it mean to be human "in fellow humanity?"

---

5. *CD* III/4, 116.

6. Ibid.

7. Ibid.

8. Christopher Chenault Roberts, *Creation and Covenant: The Significance of Sexual Difference in the Moral Theology of Marriage* (London and New York: T. & T. Clark, 2007) 143.

Simply put, that men and women are created for covenantal community attests the character of the One in whose image they are created. The triune God does not exist in splendid isolation but in radical communion and fellowship: the Godhead is three persons who indwell one another and are thus existent only as an interdependent and perichoretic fellowship.[9] Male/female relations are the place where we learn that the true form of our humanity is not autonomous or independent humanity, but rather fellow-humanity or co-humanity created for covenant in accordance with the divine likeness. In the context of relations with one another, we learn, then, that we are created for community with one another and, most importantly, with this God, Father, Son, and Holy Spirit.

It is important to acknowledge that true human being takes places as a being-in-encounter if we are to understand marriage's nature and purpose. Marriage is, as the focal point for the man/woman relationship and for our being created for covenantal community, the *center* and *end* of the man/woman relationship. I say *center* and *end* because the marital relationship "has exemplary significance for the whole relation between man and woman."[10] That it has "exemplary significance" does *not* mean that other human relationships are less valued or are less important to God or are less capable of imitating Christ. By no means: what one says of marriage can and should be said generally of the encounter of man and woman—hence the language of "exemplary significance." Just as the human relationships in general requires receiving and giving, marriage does so as well, but in a way in which something unrepeatable and incomparable takes place "between a particular man and a particular woman," namely, a complete partnership.[11] That said, not all human relationships that require receiving and giving lead to complete partnership. But because marriage aims at such a partnership it has a kind of "exemplary" significance as far as all human relationships are concerned.[12] Barth puts it this way: marriage is as "the form of the encounter of male and female in which the free, mutual, harmonious choice of love on the part of a particular man and woman leads to a *responsibly*

---

9. For a conceptual expansion of this point, see Tom Smail's most recent work, *Like Father, Like Son: The Trinity Imaged in Our Humanity* (Grand Rapids: Eerdmans, 2005).

10. *CD* III/4, 174.

11. Ibid., 182.

12. Ibid.

undertaken life."[13] What Barth is saying is that when a particular man and woman choose to love one another, marriage is considered to be the most responsible *form* of that love relation, the form in which some men and women are called to fulfill their co-humanity.

To talk about the God of the covenant and ourselves as created for covenant requires further consideration of the imperatival character of covenant language. That is, the covenant is directive of all human relationships in general. Let me explain. In marriage a way is given in which the Christian heeds the truth that she is "of one spirit" with the Lord.[14] Note that I use the language of "a way." The language of "a way" is of tremendous importance for an account of Christian marriage. To be sure, one would never want to maintain that a person who is not married is somehow less of one spirit with the Lord. By no means! Rather, it is simply to say that marriage is a matter of *vocation*. Hence the task of each person is to discern his or her "vocation with regard to the other sex."[15] Marriage is a vocation to which some are called as a result of them too being made of one spirit with the Lord in Christ Jesus, just as is celibacy. In other words, marriage in relationship to the gospel is the way in which a particular man and a particular woman live obediently in relationship to the Lord with whom they are now one in the Holy Spirit. Indeed, there is a Christian obedience that does not lead one into marriage, and there is a Christian obedience that leads one into marriage. For some, the obedience to the command of God to love God and to live as his child will entail marriage, and for others obedience to the command of God will entail being single.

This is an important point to maintain. In Western culture and in the Church in general, marriage is romanticized and sentimentalized a great deal. The Christian Church would do well to reflect upon marriage as "a special spiritual gift and vocation," rather than as a means of self-actualization, a gift in which one suffers the freedom and constraint of the Holy Spirit's sanctifying working.[16] Accordingly, marriage is indeed something that one cannot presume is just there because a man and a woman have made vows. Marriage is a gift of God appointed for some

---

13. Ibid., 140; emphasis mine.
14. 1 Cor 6:17.
15. Chenault Roberts, *Creation and Covenant*, 157.
16. *CD* III/4, 148.

such that they may live a responsibly undertaken life.[17] This life is a life of witness to God's love. In accordance with Ephesians 5, then, marriage involves "a mutual subordination for the purpose of fostering holiness, which in turn serves as a witness to Christ."[18]

To sum up this section: true human being takes place as a being in "fellow-humanity." Co-humanity or fellow-humanity means that we are created for covenantal community and for a responsibly undertaken life in relationship to one another. Such a life requires witness to God's steadfast love. A particular man and a particular woman may discover that in obedience to the command of God to be witnesses to his love, they are given a special gift and vocation, namely, the gift and vocation of marriage as a step they must take in the freedom of the Spirit such that they may truly be God's witnesses.

III

Having sketched an account of man and woman as "a being in fellow humanity" and the implications of such an account of the human being for an understanding of marriage, it is now necessary to account in greater detail for the *gift* and *vocation* of marriage.[19] I will do so *via* the following five points.

First, in marriage, as the focal point of the male/female relation, something is ventured. What is ventured is a kind of freedom that the Holy Spirit provides, such that men and women are freed *for* this "highly extraordinary fulfillment of the relation between man and woman."[20] In marriage, a particular man and a particular woman are established in a special life-partnership, which is their vocation. The vocation given to married persons, or to single persons for that matter, is the same, namely, that of "being subject to the divine command."[21] All people, whether married or single, are subject to the divine command. Some cannot be subject to this command without being married, while others can only

---

17. For a wonderful theological exploration of responsibility, see Dietrich Bonhoeffer, *Dietrich Bonhoeffer Works*, Vol. 6, *Ethics*, trans. Ilse Tödt et al., ed. Clifford J. Green (Minneapolis: Fortress, 2005) 246–98.

18. Matzko McCarthy, "Becoming One Flesh," in *Blackwell Companion*, 281.

19. These six points are a condensation of the seven Barth presents in paragraph 54 of chap XII of *CD* III/4.

20. Ibid., 184.

21. Ibid.

be truly subject to this command as married persons. Regardless, because marriage is a matter of divine vocation for some, it is, following Matt 19:1–12, "binding with all the force of divine authority, stringency, and precision."[22] In other words, marriage is an instrument that God uses to form men and women into his people, his partners, in such a way that they may more faithfully fulfill the task given to them—which is to love God and neighbor.

I would hazard a guess that this is a deeply counter-intuitive and counter-cultural way of explaining marriage's vocation. The notion of "being subject to the divine command" hardly evokes happy thoughts. Commandment sounds authoritarian, akin to an instrument of oppression, and also at times downright "male." But what I have in mind is precisely the opposite. In being subject to the commandment of God—"you will be my people"—there is freedom and life.[23] Subjection to the commandment of God as it is fulfilled in the relationship between a particular man and woman is all about a particular man and a particular woman becoming what they are—children of God. They become this in a particular relationship into which they enter as the means by which their being created for communion with God and with one other takes shape.

Second, Christian marriage functions as the "proof of love" between a husband and a wife.[24] Marriage as "a life partnership" denotes the "seriousness of love," love which is fulfilled in the form of this life-partnership.[25] The task given to a particular man and a particular woman in marriage is thus "work-labour at the work of art of their common being."[26] Their common being is not something they possess. Rather, it is a gift to them from the God who is love and whose love is their life and the basis of their partnership. Because of this, a particular man and a particular woman in marriage can never usurp their common being, but rather must see it as something toward which they must aim and something they must prove ever anew. Partnership can never be presumed, then: life-partnership is a life-long vocation. The proof of the love at the basis of marriage requires a life-time to realize.

---

22. Ibid., 185.

23. See David Novak, "Karl Barth on the Divine Command: A Jewish Response," *Scottish Journal of Theology* 54 (2001) 463–83.

24. *CD* III/4, 187.

25. Ibid.

26. Ibid., 188.

Again, the idea that marriage is a long life task devoted to the cultivation of love that lies at its core is deeply counter-intuitive. Love is commonly understood to be an individual choice that involves "the process of detachment from family, economy, and social station. . . . [Thus] The goal of a loving relationship is to have a relationship founded only on the interpersonal coupling of freely chosen partners."[27] How different is a theological understanding of love that views love as something that takes shape in "work and routine" rather than in "spontaneity and novelty," rather than as a "way of life in the community of faith."[28] Indeed, love is not a commodity to be sold and exchanged, but something that binds and constrains. Marriage, then, is rather a kind of laboratory in which love for one another is proved, love founded upon a particular man and woman being commanded to love.

Third, the task of life-partnership, which is the task of marriage, rather than being a burden, is, in theological perspective, emancipatory. Because the love that lies at marriage's basis "wills total and all-embracing fellowship for life," the man and woman of whom that total love is willed are by virtue of that love emancipated or freed to love.[29] In other words, by virtue of the love for one another that the command of God demands of them, the man and the woman become free *for* one another. At this point an analogy with Israel can be ventured. Just as Israel's freedom was dependent upon the degree to which it remained faithful to Torah and thus for Torah, so too marital partners as life-partners are free for one another inasmuch as their freedom is seen as identical with their responsibility *for* one another. To be free for one another is to be responsible for one another. Marriage is not a given, then, but rather something that "must continually become a state by the reciprocal coexistence and orientation of husband and wife in this faithfulness in love."[30] By thinking in terms of marriage as something that must continually become a state, rather than akin to something a husband and wife possess, marriage is demystified, for one is allowed to see it for what it is, namely, a life-partnership focused on a common advance toward freedom and communion with Christ. This, too, is counter-intuitive. At the heart of Christian marriage is the apocalypse of God in Christ. This

---

27. Matzko McCarthy, "Becoming One Flesh," in *Blackwell Companion*, 278.
28. Ibid., 278–79.
29. *CD* III/4, 189.
30. Ibid., 192.

apocalypse renders all human relationships transparent to itself so that they can become witnesses to God's love. The coming of God in Christ renders permeable all human relations such that they can really be relationships of genuine partnerships and faithfulness in love.

Fourth, marriage is an "exclusive life partnership."[31] What gives it its exclusive character is that it arises from and is nourished by love; but not love understood in any old way, but rather love as monogamous love. The God who establishes us as his covenant partners in our baptism directs us as his covenant partners in the ways of monogamy as particular men and women live their marriages out within the continuing life of the Church. That God directs us in the ways of monogamy is for our good. This is so because the marriage of a particular man and a particular woman is "an invitation, permission and freedom to represent and symbolize in this human form of fellowship the fellowship of God with man."[32] This summons to represent in the marital relationship the kind of love God manifests in coming to us is the occasion for conversion and renewal, as a particular man and a particular women strive to give witness to the steadfast love of God.

Fifth, marriage founded by God and lived out under his commandment "requires from both participants free and mutual love."[33] The command to love one another, to mutual love, is a command that functions as the *human* side of God's covenantal calling and gift. God's covenantal love evokes the love of a particular man and a particular women for one another as they aim at truly being each other's partner. Of course, a particular man and a particular woman can never assume that they have arrived at such a place, for if marriage is truly always becoming a state, then the love which is its basis must always be renewed. This being so, human love is at its best a reflection and never a direct representation of Jesus Christ's love for his community. "In its human basis marriage is primarily and immediately a reflection of the gracious election of the covenant, of the love of Yahweh for His people and of Jesus Christ from His community."[34] All people, whether they be married or single, are called to reflect this love in unity. It is this vocation to love, to reflect God's gracious love that unites all people in such a way that they might in an all

31. Ibid., 195.
32. Ibid., 198.
33. Ibid., 213.
34. Ibid., 215.

too frail but nonetheless real way reflect God's costly and life-giving love. Christian marriage, then, is circumscribed marriage, decentered marriage, destabilized marriage; in its very essence, it is exocentric.

Sixth and last, marriage undertaken in light of the covenant "must have the character of a responsible act outwards in relation to those around."[35] That is, marriage concluded in the sight of God is also "responsible before the Christian community."[36] It is, in David Matzko McCarthy's words, "social and productive of other mutually supporting friendships."[37] That is, marriage, if it is truly to approximate the state that God intends for it, "require[s] the faith, the preaching, the intercession, the understanding and loving interest" of the Christian community.[38] Christian marriages are in short dependent upon the Christian community, the community that baptizes into the Eucharist. For it is in the community that men and women of all ages and relational statuses hear of the summons to responsibility through the gospel of the grace of God in Jesus Christ. To the Church is revealed and given the grace of God in Christ that confers freedom. Gospel freedom is the freedom to be responsible before one another and to another in obedience to the command of God to love one another. The divine commandment pierces marriages, indeed all human relations, by summoning them out of themselves to God and thereby to the community of faith to which God is indissolubly bound. The commandment enables a marriage to be one rooted in grace and therefore humane in character, for it generates antipathy toward transgression and fosters a spirit of forgiveness in men and women who need the helping and healing grace of God in order to be complete life-partners to the one to whom they are bound.[39]

To sum up this section: marriage is self-effacing insofar as it lives not by its own story, a story that a particular man and a particular woman write about themselves, a story of self-reliance. No, Christian mar-

---

35. Ibid., 224.
36. Ibid., 228.
37. Matzko McCarthy, "Becoming One Flesh," in *Blackwell Companion*, 286.
38. *CD* III/4, 229.
39. In light of these points, can there be theological grounds upon which divorce may be the one thing necessary for a particular man and a particular woman? In short, yes. Marriage which is not real is marriage which has no divine basis and constitution. But how can one ascertain such? One cannot ascertain such in advance. As long as a particular man and a particular women cling to the promise and Yes of God in faith, a marriage has a divine basis and is therefore a real possibility.

riage, if it be worthy of the title Christian, lives by the divine faithfulness and stands in the light of it. Marriage is about God, and the love that is marriage's basis is the "specific action obedient to the commandment of God."[40]

IV

My remarks thus far have been decidedly and intentionally "Barthian" in character. It should be clear that the portrait that Barth paints for us regarding becoming one is a portrait that is deeply rooted in the Christian story. But what of a somewhat different reading of the Christian story? One of the most sophisticated and interesting pieces to appear on marriage and on why marriage is about two bodies, and not necessarily two bodies of differing sexes, is by Graham Ward, a distinguished British Anglican theologian with strong "postmodern" leanings. I introduce Ward at this point for he is one who takes with utmost seriousness many of Barth's basic insights, but then argues that the conclusions that Barth reaches regarding why marriage is between a particular man and a particular woman, rather than being a matter of two bodies coming together in such a way that each is truly *for* the other, are not in line with Barth's own deepest insights. In other words, Ward uses Barth to critique Barth so as to render Barth's account of marriage more consistent with Barth's own deepest insights.

My point in discussing Ward's very sophisticated proposals is not to engage in finer points of Barth interpretation *per se*, but to show that one can at many points make a convincing theological case for why the account of marriage sketched above can be expanded beyond a "particular man" and a "particular woman" to be that of two persons of the same sex. In short, the problem with the account as sketched above would, according to Ward, be that it "privileges one form of relationship over another, constructs gender along the lines of biological, reproductive difference."[41] In other words, Ward says that Barth does not take adequately seriously the extent to which the gospel deconstructs and disrupts assumed understandings of sex, sexual identities, and, especially, gender. Likewise, Barth does not take seriously enough, in Ward's judgment, the oppressive features that inhere in accounts of the male and female that are supposedly rooted in natural—biological—difference.

---

40. *CD* III/4, 218.
41. Graham Ward, *Cities of God* (New York and London: Routledge, 2000) 183.

Let me recount Ward's basic arguments for a moment. Ward postulates that we must read sexual difference theologically rather than biologically: "Representations of sexual difference can too easily become embroiled in, and reduced to, chromosological differences—even when this is not intended."[42] Stated somewhat differently, Ward is making the case that "bodies are not self-grounded and self-defining."[43] This is Ward's way of moving beyond the polarity of biological essentialism and social constructivism. Accordingly, maleness and femaleness cannot be reified, for maleness and femaleness are performed within a "social context and an historical movement that causes the meaning attached to those nouns to exceed their biological [and social] definitions."[44] Indeed, maleness and femaleness—in short, sexual difference—do not only thus exceed anatomical, social, and linguistic reference—sexuality, gender, personhood are all deemed by Ward to be largely "symbolic."[45] The symbolic character of human sexuality, gender, and personhood indicates that they are that which must be practiced—they "are all practices."[46]

To be sure, Ward does "get" Barth and "gets" him well. Ward's basic concern is that Barth reduces maleness and femaleness to biology. Barth, in other words, operates with a *natural* rather than a *revealed* understanding of sexuality and gender and thereby what it means to be male and female. Hence Ward argues that Barth's antipathy toward homosexual practice is precisely because Barth has not followed his own deepest insights, which in this case would require that "our knowledge of what is natural and social has to be a knowledge revealed to us by God."[47] Thus Ward argues that to the extent that one works with a revealed understanding, the mystery of same-sex relationships open up. So Ward: "Same-sex relationships displace . . . heterosexist symbolics, revealing a love which exceeds biological reproduction. . . . Attraction arises still in difference, in opposition, through alterity. . . . But exactly what is other in a relationship between two 'women' or two 'men' becomes less easy to define, to catalogue."[48] Thus, homosexual and heterosexual relation-

---

42. Ward, *Cities*, 186.
43. Ibid., 63.
44. Ibid., 64–65.
45. Ibid., 64–65.
46. Ibid., 69.
47. Ibid., 197.
48. Ibid., 200.

ships are not so easily designated. Indeed, agapeic love, united as it is with erotic love, is not captive to biology, to reproduction, or to a person of the opposite sex. For "true desire, that is, God-ordained desire can only be heterosexual," writes Ward. That is, God-ordained desire is as such insofar as one desires another who remains other. But for Ward neither heterosexual nor homosexual relationships have an *a priori* advantage when it comes to becoming a truly heterosexual relationship, that is, a relationship saturated with true desire *for* the other and thus for God.

What then of marriage as involving, as I have assumed, a particular man and a particular woman? Ward argues, "Marriage is the narrative of the creative interval between two bodies, maintained by the labor of loving as it moves in hope towards the eschatological coming of the Kingdom, which is redemption."[49] In other words, marriage is about two bodies moving toward God's personally and ecclesially redemptive future, which is all about two bodies whose structure of desire is heterosexual—that is, desire *for* the other. It follows then that difference, as ingredient in this "creative interval," is that which ought to be blessed and sanctified by the church. Accordingly, difference is a good that must be discerned, and when found, blessed. Marriages composed of two persons of the same sex or of a different sex are, in Ward's judgment, equally capable of manifesting difference and thereby genuine *kenotic* desire that is rooted in desire for God and God's desire for us.[50] In sum, Ward writes, "The Church must sanctify, then, genuine sexual difference through its liturgies—whether that sexual difference is evident between two women, two men or a man and a woman."[51] Difference cannot be reduced to chromosological differences. Alterity is what matters, and alterity cannot be parsed along biological lines, but rather transcends the biological inasmuch as genuine kenotic desire for the other is concerned.

Having sketched Ward's proposals, let me raise a few brief comments, both positive and negative, in relationship to them. In terms of the positive, what is most helpful is that Ward's account takes very seriously the disruptive and, dare I say, apocalyptic nature of the triune God's saving grace. By this I mean that Ward appreciates that all general conceptions, definitions, and ideas of what it means to be human, to

---

49. Ibid., 202.

50. It should be noted that this is evidence of the Augustinian spirit of Ward's proposals.

51. Ward, *Cities*, 202.

be male and female, to be creatures created in the *imago dei*, cannot simply be assumed to be transparent to revealed truth. Indeed, genuine humanity, which is always co-humanity, that is, humanity existing kenotically, ought to be mapped in relationship to basic christological, ecclesiological, and eschatological doctrine if one is to arrive at a truthful account of humanity.

In terms of critical comments, I wonder, first, to what extent Ward operates with a sufficiently Christian understanding of sexual *desire*. Does Ward apply to "desire" or "difference" the crucial insight that he receives from Barth, namely, that what constitutes true desire must proceed on the basis of *revealed* understanding? It seems as if Ward reifies and objectifies desire in such a way that desire and also difference themselves become the ultimate good and therefore impervious to self-criticism. Commenting on Ward, Chenault Roberts writes, "He [Ward] assumes where there is desire there must be theologically significant difference and does not interrogate same-sex desire at any point, asking if it might be post-lapsarian in origin and hence, unlike sexual difference, possibly testifying to sin and not to ontologically significant differences."[52] That Ward makes this kind of move is because he has not, in my judgment, offered an adequate account of the *imago dei*. If, as Ward insists, "sexual difference . . . constitutes we human creatures as the *imago dei*," and sexual difference endorses both the separation and relation of bodies, can an account of the *imago dei*—revealed as both male and female—no longer take biological differences into account?[53] What such a question raises is indeed a basic concern, namely, the extent to which Ward's proposals de-emphasize creation, thereby casting aside biological and, therewith, sexual difference.

To be sure, our own conceptions of maleness and femaleness are laden with cultural and historical determinants, but I cannot help but think that *imago dei* language would have us affirm something other than simply the idea that marriage denotes a narrative of two bodies marked by kenotic love rather than the bodies of sexually differentiated human beings. Indeed, marriage is earthy business, material business, and the human bodies of men and women created in the image of God are indicative of an "irreversible structural human differentiation" that an account of marriage circumscribed by God's covenant must honor.

---

52. Chenault Roberts, *Creation and Covenant*, 197.
53. Ward, *Cities*, 55.

Bodies are not something to which one can attach "so much symbolism," as does Ward.[54]

Second, I wonder where the Bible fits into all of this. Ward's proposals are very thin, exegetically speaking. While I do not want and do not demand from him prooftexts, I do think that exegesis of Holy Scripture is necessary.[55] Indeed, I would be most grateful to Ward if he engaged in theological exegesis so that I might know what to do with Jesus's own words that seem to reiterate the normativity of sexual union between male and female in Matt 19:16. Likewise, I would like to see him read Paul, specifically Paul's carrying over in Romans 1 of the rabbinical texts against homosexual practice rooted in the holiness codes of Leviticus 17–18. The paucity of theological exegesis of Holy Scripture leaves me wondering why Ward would not at least attempt to read Scripture in a way that complements his creative and critical reinhabitation of Barth and puts his considerable intellectual and theological acumen to further work.

In short, I find myself critical of Ward's proposals is because he has not given me a theologically adequate account of sexual difference in the marriage relationship and of that difference as being ingredient in the *imago dei*. That is to say, the polarity present in terms of a differentiated oneness in marriage between a given man and woman is participant in an even more elemental polarity, namely, the Creator/creature distinction. The Creator—the triune God—has established the most intimate communion with the creature, but has done so in a way that maintains God's own difference and qualitative distinction from the creature. But in so doing, God has called men and women to emulate the inner dynamics of God's triune life in and through their differences as men and women in such a way that they too may be witnesses to God's own form of relational life. Indeed, unity includes distinction, and I would argue that Ward's view of difference does not take adequately seriously the kind of sexual difference that marriage presupposes and requires and that nurtures true desire—desire for the other who remains other—at the materially differentiated level. Accordingly, marriage presupposes the kind of alterity ingredient in our being created as male and female in the image of God, which is a kind of alterity at the creaturely level

---

54. Chenault Roberts, *Creation and Covenant*, 149, 194.

55. See further Tim Perry, "Learning to Fly: Radical Orthodoxy, Graham Ward, and the Renewal of Anglican Theology," *Canadian Evangelical Review* 22 (2005) 15–31.

not exhausted by chromosological differences, but is nonetheless mindful of them and thus of creation in general, and thus embraces the givenness of creation as the "material presupposition for the covenant," the covenant that effects the kind of unity-in-distinction between God and creates the genuine form of humanity as co-humanity that is the goal of Christ's redemptive work.[56]

In short, my concern with Ward is that he renders maleness and femaleness as no longer "a necessary relation."[57] This is problematic because in sexual difference we learn not only our interdependence with respect to one another but also our distinctness. Our being created sexually different as male and female cannot then be de-emphasized; for our creation—the corporeal shape of our humanity as sexually differentiated human beings—attests our being created for covenant with God. To be created for covenant with the triune God is to be created for co-humanity, that is, created as men and women who have a vocation with respect to one another, and whose vocation as men and women is most fulfilled in relationship to those of the opposite sex. Only such relations truthfully witness to the reality-in-difference that is true of the inner life of the triune God.

V

To conclude, marriage is *not* first and foremost about us, but about the triune God. But because it is about this God, it is also about us as those to whom this God has freely bound himself in the resurrected Jew Jesus. The God of the gospel is especially concerned with restoring men and women to life in communion with himself. Marriage serves as an instrument through which God calls particular men and women created in his image to respond to their sexual difference such that they may better fulfill the vocation common to all baptized persons: love of God and neighbor. Accordingly, marriage is a *sign* of God's costly covenantal love, the purpose of which is to witness to God's love in a way that is not only exemplified in the love of a particular man and a particular woman for one another, but is also faithful to the Christian community and to the call given to the community to make disciples of all nations.

---

56. Chenault Roberts, *Creation and Covenant*, 195.
57. Ibid., 196.

8

Forbid Them Not

The Place of Children in a Theology of Marriage

Tim Perry

In the consumer-driven and oriented culture of the contemporary West, children are a bit of an enigma. On the one hand, there has never been a generation that has idealized and indeed idolized youth, and childhood in particular, as ours has. Children have rights—as my six year-old son regularly reminds me—rights Western governments are determined rightly to protect. Children are protected from lead paint, bicycle falls, and playground accidents of various sorts in ways and means unheard of when I was a child. When I rode my lead-painted bicycle without helmet or supervision to disappear for hours in the woods and fields behind my house no one seemed to mind. Not so today. Our collective concern for child safety was brilliantly satirized in an episode of *The Simpsons* entitled, "Bye Bye Nerdie."[1] Having heard of the countless household threats to babies, Homer starts his own baby-proofing business only to find that his tips and products cause the collapse of the baby injury related businesses in Springfield. Homer therefore closes his business and the economy of Springfield is restored.

---

1. John Frink and Don Payne, "Bye Bye Nerdie," *The Simpsons*, Episode 263. Originally aired on Fox Television, March 11, 2001.

Homer's baby business also gets us to the dark side of this hyper-reactivity. As much as it does reflect legitimate concern for child welfare, there can be no doubt that the child-safety industry displays just how much children have become objectified in the late modern West. They are not so much human beings in their own right as they are objects of desire, canvasses upon which we might paint our latest consumer-driven dreams. And of course, such canvasses must be protected—for *our* sakes (thus, cross-culturally adopted children are the latest accessories for the power couple that has everything). But, of course, the converse is also true. If, for the sake of satisfying adults' desires, children are to be prematurely sexualized, then, with the exception of what falls under the umbrella of sexual abuse, they are.

Perhaps the most tragic instance of this instrumentalization of children is disclosed when we try to discern the reasons for our switch from the language of "unborn infant" to the far less human and far more clinical "fetus." While a thorough examination would take me far away from the purpose of my essay, I would not be surprised to find out that, in the vast majority of cases, the move in language is not based at all on any scientific determinations about whether the human being so described can, say, feel pain, or some other empirically verifiable watershed. Rather, I would expect that the data would show that the change in language is determined by what adults intend to do with the human being we have thus labeled. Few if any medical interventions will be spared to save the life of an unborn infant, while, perhaps in the next operating room, a fetus with a better chance of surviving will be aborted. Children—whether desired or discarded—have become a consumer item in late modernity. In the late modern imagination, children are objects.

Fortunately, cautions about the objectification of children are being made increasingly in the guilds of academic and pastoral theology. Indeed, theologies of children and childhood represent a new and burgeoning field in theological literature, with book-length works emerging only within the last eight to ten years.[2] Theologians and Christian ethicists from across the theological spectrum—though I must say that

---

2. See, e.g., Angela Shier-Jones, ed., *Children of God: Towards a Theology of Childhood* (Peterborough: Epworth, 2007); Odd Magne Bakke, *When Children Became People: The Birth of Childhood in Early Christianity* (Minneapolis: Fortress, 2005); Bonnie J. Miller-McLemore, *Let the Children Come: Re-Imagining Childhood from a Christian Perspective* (San Francisco: Jossey Bass, 2003); Marcia J. Bunje, ed., *The Child in Christian Thought* (Grand Rapids: Eerdmans, 2001).

in the course of preparing this article, I have found that feminist theologians are the most trenchant in their observations and criticism—are voicing concerns about how children have gone from being idealized to idolized to being, now, consumable.[3] Christians across the theological and confessional and denominational divides, I hope, will welcome and take seriously the prophetic challenges these writers lay not simply at the world out there, but at the feet of Christian parents who have in many ways subtly been co-opted by this way of thinking.

I do not pretend to be an expert in this field, and I would not be surprised to find out that the observation I am about to make would need nuancing in the light of further research. But I am going to make it anyway. As I prepared this paper, I was struck by how little of this theological literature actually treated children alongside, or perhaps within a larger discussion of, Christian marriage. Children were spoken of as gifts, as sinners, and as bearers of the image of God. Theological categories were applied to various stages of life from conception through adolescence. All of that was good. Very little of the reading I did, however, centered on children as, well, children; as human beings in the care of parents, or more particularly, as boys and girls being raised by mothers and fathers;[4] as part of a theologically robust account of marriage.

Of course, this is not to say that, theologically, discussion of children only belongs within a discussion of marriage. Jesus, after all, had a great deal to say about children and none of it, as far as I know, arose

---

3. A colleague suggested here that children were as much consumers as consumable in late modern culture. Of course, that suggestion is right. But the construction of child as consumer is, of course, not of the child's own making and thus underscores my point.

4. The distinctions between "children" and "boys and girls" and "parents" and "mothers and fathers" might seem at first glance to involve a minimal move from the general to the particular. That is true, but there is something more fundamental at stake. In Canada, we have moved in four decades from Pierre Trudeau's dictum that the state has no business in the bedrooms of the nation to a new social experiment in which that state has taken up residence not simply in the bedroom but in the bed, wishing by judicial fiat to (re-)define those relationships found there—spouse, parent, child—regardless of the welfare of those particular boys, girls, mothers, and fathers so redefined. The notion that the state can and should define relationships it did not create is an assertion of raw power without precedent in legal or political tradition used to buttress a new and dangerous social experiment against which the Church will be forced to take a stand of prophetic witness in the years ahead. See Douglas Farrow, *Nation of Bastards: Essays on the End of Marriage* (Toronto: BPS, 2007). On the relationship between power and tradition in the task of law-making in politics, see Oliver O'Donovan, *The Ways of Judgment* (Grand Rapids: Eerdmans, 2005).

out of a discussion of marriage. Paul and the rest of the New Testament writers have very little to say about children whether within marriage or somewhere else. But, having granted that there are other important theological loci in which children will arise as a subject of reflection, may it not also be said that to have nothing to say about children within marriage is, well, odd?

Which brings me round to the thesis for my paper. It is this: *Children and their procreation are necessary, though not exhaustive, subsets of a Christian theology of marriage.* Or, conversely, *our understanding of marriage will remain at best impoverished or at worst narcissistic and even Gnostic if it does not at some point include reflection on children and procreation.* I will, in the light of Dr. Radner's essay (chapter 5 in this volume), only touch briefly on matters of procreation; I will focus instead on children once they have arrived.

I cannot in the space provided demonstrate this thesis as fully as some readers might like; rather, I will work toward the lower aim of showing it to be at least plausible and therefore worthy of further consideration in the following steps. First, I will reflect on the aforementioned silence, especially as it has evidenced itself in a recent Anglican discussion of marriage, namely, the St. Michael Report. I will suggest that the reason for silence—the experience of modern Canadian Anglicans—is theologically inadequate. I will end the section, though, by suggesting that there is a very good historical reason for Christian theologians if not to be quiet, then at least to be circumspect when it comes to children.

That caution will serve as the key boundary in my second section, when I begin to sketch what a theology of children within marriage might look like. Here I will base my remarks heavily on the work of Karl Barth and his discussion of parents and children in *Church Dogmatics* III/4. I hope to show how Barth's conception of humanity as beings-in-relation and beings-for-others is played out in the unique relationship that exists between parents and children. Finally, in my third section, I will suggest ways in which that essentially covenantal understanding of parents and children in relation enriches our theology of marriage by forcing it, in ways both wondrous and not, to embrace the sheer messiness and materiality of human love as the sacrament of the divine self-giving of Christ for the Church.

ON NOT TALKING ABOUT CHILDREN

Above, I noted an odd silence with respect to marriage in the growing theological literature concerned with children and childhood. In this first section, I want to look at a discussion of marriage that reflects this silence. The *Report of the Primate's Theological Commission of the Anglican Church of Canada on the Blessing of Same Sex Unions*, or *The Saint Michael Report*[5] is, unlike much of the contemporary discussion, from first to last both theological and distinctively Anglican. As such, it deserves to be taken very seriously by all parties at this consultation as sketching the kind of theological case that must be made by the supporters of the blessing of same-sex unions if the Canadian Church is finally to undertake the venture.

That, it seems to me, is the key to the entire document. It is not a conclusive statement on the matter as much as it is a careful, nuanced plea for the whole of our church to consider carefully how the blessing of same-sex unions might impinge upon other theological considerations in doctrines of "salvation, incarnation, the person and work of the Holy Spirit, theological anthropology, sanctification, and holy matrimony" (*Overview*, 10). There is a deep wisdom in these remarks. Even if the blessing of same-sex unions is not a creedal or core matter, it does bear upon and reflect certain commitments in other creedal matters. And these matters ought to be theologically addressed before a sound decision can be made.

I therefore am very happy that the last General Synod received the *Saint Michael Report* even as I am not as happy about the way in which some of its detractors—on the right and on the left—have spoken about it, both before and after. For even if it is not a perfect document (and I have my own reasons for thinking so), it is a very helpful one insofar as it maps the theological terrain that will need to be covered in order for decisions to be made with theological integrity at the next General Synod. I know many Anglicans are wary of their theologians. From across the church, many would echo the observation of the character in the wonderful satire *Yes Prime Minister*, Sir Humphrey Appleby: "Theology is a device for enabling agnostics to stay within the church,"[6] and therefore

---

5. *Report of the Primate's Theological Commission of the Anglican Church of Canada on the Blessing of Same Sex Unions*. Online: http://www2.anglican.ca/primate/ptc/smr.htm, April 9, 2008. Paragraphs are cited parenthetically in the text.

6. Antony Jay and Jonathan Lynn, "The Bishop's Gambit," *Yes Prime Minister*, Episode 7. Originally aired on the BBC, February 20, 1986.

to be avoided by the majority of believers, clergy and lay. Nevertheless, we in the Canadian church would do well to heed the cautions of our theologians who, while they disagree profoundly about the desired outcome, seem to me to agree that the worst way to go about this decision is the way we're going about it: namely, to create facts on the ground only to think them through theologically afterward, if at all.

But back to the subject at hand: children. I find it odd that in a document that is so carefully considered, children get such little treatment. They are explicitly mentioned only in paragraph 31, which is worth quoting in full:

> Questions have been raised about whether this complementarity of male and female is necessary for every godly human sexual relationship. Each person, whether male or female, is made in God's own image. Some, we know, are sexually attracted to persons of their own gender. While same gender couples cannot procreate naturally, they are able to contribute to the community in which they live, and it is possible for them either to adopt children, or, for some, to use artificial insemination or *in vitro* fertilization. While in earlier ages the greatest evidence of God's blessing was deemed to be the gift of children, procreation is no longer portrayed as the primary end of marriage in our Anglican liturgies of holy matrimony (*Book of Common Prayer*, p. 170; *Book of Alternative Services* p. 528). Healthy, heterosexual Anglican couples may, and some do, decide not to have children. Such relationships bear fruit in community service, Christian ministries, and the pursuit of holiness. Does the lack of gender complementarity in homosexual Anglican couples hinder them from making the same commitment to one another in the eyes of God and in the view of the Christian community? Such same-sex relationships, founded upon mutual dedication and love, seek God's blessing upon their life together, to the exclusion of all others, until parted by death. Thus the Commission understands the blessing that they seek to be analogous to that received in Christian matrimony, rather than, for example, the blessing of a house or home. The question that remains is whether the lack of complementarity of gender in same-sex unions can prevent such a couple from being a means of grace, experiencing spiritual growth, and participating in the life of God. (31)

This paragraph follows a discussion of sexual difference as the sign of "human being in relation" that is the foundation of marriage and precedes a discussion of the challenges associated with thinking theologically about family—especially as family defined by blood is relativized in the New Testament by a family defined by water, bread, and wine. Which leads me to point out the obvious strength of the paragraph: this is exactly the place where discussion of children should come up. And it does.

It is also, however, incomplete. It acknowledges the reality of some heterosexual marriages that are childless, whether because of a physical lack of capacity or by choice, and the fact that others conceive children in medically extraordinary ways and still others choose to adopt. It states quite rightly that childless relationships nevertheless may "bear fruit" in other ways and in such ways, genuinely reflect the pursuit of holiness. The paragraph then calls into question the liturgies of holy matrimony when they express the view that procreation is the primary end of marriage.[7] Of course, these acknowledgements may drive a wedge between procreation and marriage that allows space to ask whether other sexual yet non-procreative relationships may be recognized as means of grace that merit church blessing. These are right and fine questions to pose. Yet, it seems to me that more questions need to be raised here.

Specifically, I believe the following questions have been passed over. Even if the procreation of children is not to be perceived to be the primary end of marriage, is the contemporary experience of the faithful a sufficient theological basis for saying so? Might it not be that the procreation of children, even if not the primary end of marriage, discloses

---

7. The notion of procreation being primary is a hallmark of the Western tradition. It seems to be found in Augustine, when he writes, "Therefore the good of marriage throughout all nations and all men stands in the occasion of begetting, and faith of chastity: but, so far as pertains unto the People of God, also in the sanctity of the Sacrament . . ." *On the Good of Marriage*, 32 in *Nicene and Post-Nicene Fathers*, vol. 3 (New York: Christian Literature Publishing, 1890). Online: http://www.ccel.org/ccel/schaff/npnf103.html. Thomas Aquinas similarly affirms that "it is clear that 'offspring' is the most essential thing in marriage, secondly 'faith,' and thirdly 'sacrament;' even as to man it is more essential to be in nature than to be in grace, although it is more excellent to be in grace." Thomas Aquinas, *The Summa Theolgica of Saint Thomas Aquinas*, IIIb.49.3, trans. Fathers of the English Domincan Province (New York: Benzinger, 1947). Online: http://www.ccel.org/ccel/aquinas/summa.XP.ii.XP_Q49.XP_Q49_A3.html. This finds modern expression in the *Catechism of the Catholic Church*, § 1652: "By its very nature the institution of marriage and married love is ordered to the procreation and education of the offspring and it is in them that it finds its crowning glory." The Canadian *Book of Common Prayer* affirms the first two in *The Form of Solemnization of Matrimony*. See *The Book of Common Prayer* (Toronto: Anglican Book Centre, 1962) 564. In a private conversation, Oliver O'Donovan suggested provocatively that the ordering of procreation, fidelity, sacrament for Augustine is one of *ascending* importance whereas the Western tradition generally has treated it as one of *descending* importance.

truths about the nature of humanity, as being in covenantal relation with God and each other, that cannot simply be passed over? If so, what truths are disclosed? Now, I do not think it is the responsibility of the *Saint Michael Report* to answer these questions. Rather, I think it ought to have raised them as questions deserving further exploration.

I will take up such exploration in the second and third sections of this paper. Before I do, though, I want to make perfectly clear that there is good reason for theologians to be reticent about children and good reason for such reticence marking our discussions. We can get at that reticence if we ask ourselves just where the notion of childhood as commodity came from.

The culprits, tragically, are us. The post-Christian commoditization of children is the bastard of liberal Protestant thinking on children from the first half of the twentieth century. The reduction of Christian eschatology to the inevitable progress toward the humanly attainable kingdom of God transformed children into the vehicles through which that kingdom would arrive. Thus, it was not Christ who was the hope of the world according to the slogan of the 1954 Methodist national conference on family life, but "the Christian Family."[8]

The eschatological hope of the kingdom, as Amy Laura Hall painstakingly shows in her book *Conceiving Parenthood: American Protestantism and the Spirit of Reproduction*, was slowly downloaded on to Christian parents, who became morally obligated to have well planned, properly cared for, clean, and, if necessary, medicated children. It was an often unspoken, but no less real moral obligation for such children to be carefully segregated from others who were unplanned, untended, unclean, and unmedicated.

And it is striking to see (this is no metaphor, for Hall's work is done through an analysis of largely visual images in Christian popular publications) how this segregation is visualized by advertisers of products ranging from kitchen appliances to drugs. The children from which the Christian mother is to keep her own are, almost always, the children of the maid—who is most often African-American, though sometimes an immigrant. The segregation was defined, in other words, in terms of class and race. Christians thus not only divided children between those perceived as chosen and those just occurring through default, they defined

---

8. Amy Laura Hall, *Conceiving Parenthood: American Protestantism and the Spirit of Reproduction* (Grand Rapids: Eerdmans, 2007) 14–16.

the chosen children in terms of what they would do. Properly planned and prepared, they would be the vehicles through which the kingdom would come.

I suggest that when we look at the post-Christian consumerization of children as objects, we see a post-Christian realized eschatology brought to life like Frankenstein's monster. Children are no longer valued as the vehicles through which we will bring in the kingdom. Our day is far less optimistic than it was sixty years ago. But children's value is still defined not in terms of their intrinsic worth as human beings, themselves images of God, but in terms of how they will make adults' lives more manageable, happier; in terms of what they accomplish for us (lest any think that I am overdrawing the case, by the way, I would invite you carefully to consider Hall's detailed analysis of liberal Protestant complicity in eugenics, abortion, and the psychotropic medication of children, complicity in decisions regarding what kinds of children deserve what kind of life or even life *tout simple*).

It may be, then, in the providence of God, a blessing that Protestant theologians have had relatively little to say about childhood for the last fifty years. After all, part of the dilemma Christians face over the instrumentalization and consumerization of children today is of our own making. The question hanging over the remainder of this paper, then, is "Have we learned from that terrible and costly mistake?" Are we willing, as Hall asks, to reject the heritage of liberal Protestantism (ironically enough, a heritage that appears alive and well in the family values rhetoric of contemporary conservative Protestantism) and commit the supposedly cardinal sin of "ecclesial miscegenation"—to preach the gospel to all and band whosoever comes into communities for the pursuit of holiness? That question will serve as a boundary as I try to move past the silence in our own church and reflect upon children within the context of marriage.

BARTH ON PARENTS AND CHILDREN

With that caution in mind, let us turn to more constructive matters. To lay the groundwork for the questions of section 3 to be taken up, I will turn to Karl Barth's treatment of parents and children in *Church Dogmatics* III/4.[9] This may require a word of explanation. Why turn here? After all,

---

9. Karl Barth, *Church Dogmatics*, vol. III/4, *The Doctrine of Creation*, ed. T. F. Torrance and G. W. Bromiley (Edinburgh: T. & T. Clark, 1958) 242–83 (Hereafter *CD* III/4).

the reception of Barth in Anglican churches has been mixed. In part, I must confess that the Barthian turn reflects my own sympathies and expertise. But there is more to it than what may be my own theological idiosyncrasies. I turn to Barth for two reasons.

First, I do so to honor the intensions of the framers of this consultation. Barth's treatment of parents and children is an extended reflection on Eph 6:1–4: "Children, obey your parents in the Lord, for this is right. 'Honor your mother and father' (this is the first commandment with a promise), 'that it may be well with you and that you may live long on the earth.' Fathers, do not provoke your children to anger, but bring them up in the discipline and instruction of the Lord." And this Pauline restatement of the fifth commandment (Deut 5:16) in the light of the gospel follows directly from the passage that forms the basis for the marriage track of this consultation (namely, Eph 5:21–33). Indeed, as both Professors Jeal and Radner argue elsewhere in this volume, to stop our exegesis of the nuptial mystery at 5:33, as though children are tacked on as an otherwise unnecessary appendage, is simply not true to what Paul had (and has) to say.

Second, in turning to Barth, I also wish to remain plowing in the furrows of *The Saint Michael Report*, which, especially in its reflections under the rubric, "Human Relationships and Sanctification" (§§30–37), appears to me to have been influenced by key themes in Barth's theological anthropology. In turning to Barth to ground our talk about children, I am hoping to suggest that even as I am pushing the report, I am pushing in accord with its own intentions.

The place to begin is with Barth's insistence that the human being is never a solitary individual, but is always a being-in-relation. And in the first instance, that relation is a covenant partnership with God through God's gracious election of humanity in and through Jesus Christ. The first instance of being-in-relation then is not biological, as though beings, whether in relation as male and female or parents and children, defined the covenant. In Barth's mind, this would be the worst sort of natural theology. Rather, human beings, covenanted to God through Christ, exhibit this covenantal relation in their creaturely nature: in the

---

The secondary literature on Barth is large and increasing exponentially as his significance as a theologian becomes clearer now forty years after his death. In my judgment, one of the best introductions to his doctrine of creation—in which our discussion falls—is Kathryn Tanner, "Creation and Providence," in *The Cambridge Companion to Karl Barth*, ed. John Webster (Cambridge: Cambridge University Press, 2000) 111–26.

union of difference of man and woman and in the procreation of children to which such union normally leads. Behind the relation of male and female and subsequently, parents and children, there is the relation of God to God's people in Christ that is itself grounded in God's triune identity as the One who Loves in Freedom. The covenant, in other words, is prior to and reflected in creation.

What happens when this insight is brought to bear specifically on the relation of parents and children? Well, first, it establishes the relation as one of authority. "Children obey your parents," says the apostle, echoing the Torah. But the authority so established is, second, not an absolute authority. Children are to obey their parents "in the Lord" even as fathers are to exercise discipline without provoking wrath. The notions that loyalty to God may take precedence over loyalty to parents, and that the gospel constricts the ways in which the raising of children can be done, relativize the authority of the *paterfamilias* in ways that would have been understood to be radical for the first hearers of Paul's words.

For Barth, the gospel discloses that parental authority is not grounded in biology, chronology, or morality. Rather, "the decisive action for which the parents are responsible in relation to their children, and which the latter must be content to accept, is primarily and properly God's action, which their human action can only attest."[10] Barth affirms parental authority insofar as it does legitimate the view that in children's eyes, parents have a "Godward aspect, and are for them God's natural and primary representatives."[11] Because the biological relation—a relation in place and intact without regard to the child's choice—the chronological relation and the moral relation (i.e., hopefully, parents are more advanced in virtue) are, in the economy of grace, signs pointing to the being and act of God, children are to respond to parents with honor and obedience. Thus, parental authority is established by the gracious command of God.

By grounding the relation in the divine, however, parental authority is also relativized both "vertically" and "horizontally."[12] Vertically, authority is relativized by the insistence that even as from the child's

---

10. *CD* III/4, 247.

11. Ibid., 241.

12. The language is drawn from William Werpehowski, "Reading Karl Barth on Children," in *The Child in Christian Thought*, ed. Marcia J. Bunge (Grand Rapids: Eerdmans, 2001) 395.

perspective parents are God's representatives, parents are not to view themselves as such.[13] Rather, parents are to regard their roles as that of "elders" charged "to imitate God's action, and, insofar as they do so in all honesty, the children are summoned to honour God by honouring parents, by being content to accept this action of their parents."[14]

Horizontally, the relationship is relativized by the use of the term just mentioned: "elders." It is striking that Barth has chosen an ecclesiological rather than biological term to describe parental authority from the parents' perspective. In this way, Barth observes that childless couples and adoptive parents may be called to exercise parental authority even as the "Godward aspect" tied to biological procreation must always in some sense remain unique.[15] I need to say a brief word on this notion of uniqueness. Those who (either happily or unhappily) read Barth as obliterating biology, when he speaks about men and women or parents and children, leave me discomfited. Barth reads creation christologically and therefore eschatologically, to be sure. Creation is always seen in Christ and therefore seen as always becoming New Creation. But it is still a doctrine of creation. Barth does have his faults. But an incipient Marcionism or Manichaeism, at least as far as I can tell, is not one of them.

Barth elaborates horizontal relativization further in a meditation on the story of Jesus at the Temple (Luke 2:41–51).[16] Jesus's apparent rebuke of his mother's concern, "Why were you searching for me? Did you not know that I must be in my Father's house?" does look like a dishonoring of the Lord's parents. Not only did he stay in Jerusalem without their permission or knowledge, with these words he appears to upbraid them for worrying after his welfare. To perceive this story as weakening or suspending Jesus's relationship to his parents or their authority over him, however, is gravely to misunderstand it. Rather, it shows that Mary and Joseph had indeed fulfilled the "Godward aspect" of their parental calling by training the child Jesus to obey the first commandment above all others, including the command to honor them.

---

13. *CD* III/4, 278–79. This, in Barth's view, would violate the first commandment (cf. Barth, *CD* III/4, 251–52).
14. *CD* III/4, 247.
15. Ibid., 268. Cf. Werpehowski, "Reading Karl Barth on Children," 396 n. 37.
16. *CD* III/4, 249–50.

Therefore, Jesus's action is rightly understood as honoring his parents even if they did not immediately perceive it as such. Mary, Luke says especially, even as she did not understand Jesus's words, kept and treasured them. This suggests that, at some point in the future, she came to understand just how the rebuke honored her authority and Joseph's over the Lord as he grew in wisdom and stature. This is borne out by the story's conclusion, in which the adolescent Jesus returns with his parents to Nazareth and submits again to them (2:51).

Such instances, says Barth, wherein the believer is called to obey God *more than* other humans (cf. Acts 5:29—the text does not say "rather than") may well bring real and painful conflict, but the child is not so much called out from under the command to honor his or her parents, as he is called by God to honor them in ways they do not understand (cf. Luke 2:19; 50). The command to honor—even when relativized—is left intact even when it becomes apparent to children that their parents are not only elders, but also imperfect and even sinners.[17]

To now, we have looked at the relationship from the perspective of the child (children obey your parents). If this perspective sees the relationship in terms of honor and obedience, considered from the perspective of the parent the relationship is one of mediating God's promise ("that it may be well with you"). How ought parents to love their children in such a way as to bear witness to the promise that relativizes their own authority and establishes genuine human freedom?[18] To that question we now turn.

First, parental love is to be grounded in, point to, and pervaded with the free love of God. Barth writes: "Parents live for their children as they stand before them in the confidence that God is the One who undertakes for their children as for themselves, that He is their Advocate and Guardian, that He is the One who truly lives for them. And that the parents, with all that they can be and do, are only His witnesses."[19] As a witness of the divine love, parental love is called to be unconditional and realistic. Unconditional in the sense that parents will not "control and mould the lives" of their children according to their own; realistic in

---

17. Ibid., 257.

18. Of course, by freedom, Barth does not mean *autonomy* in contemporary sense of the word. Freedom is always freedom *for* obedience to the divine command and *alongside* others called into covenant fellowship in and through Jesus Christ.

19. *CD* III/4, 279.

the sense that they will not "smooth out all their paths, to clear away all obstacles to their progress."[20] Indeed so to stamp or insulate the lives of our children, says Barth, is nothing but a "mimicry of love."[21]

Second, parents will love their children in and through the exercise of authority over them. Again, however, this authority is grounded in and accordingly relativized by its witness to the authority of God as disclosed in the gospel. Thus, it is not a "domestic hierarchy" based on an "invented picture of superiority and inferiority." It is a relationship grounded "in the Lord." Nor is it an authority grounded in the sheer exercise of parental will or the desire to command. Such a relationship, defined in terms of a naked assertion of law and judgment, is precisely that which provokes children to wrath. Rather, parental authority is "exercised as the children realize that the parents, like themselves, stand under an authority, i.e., that they live under an immediate and unconditional majesty and power." The legitimacy of parental authority exists only insofar as it points away from itself to the authority of the One who loves in freedom.

Accordingly, third, the raising of children is not to be done under either loose or severe disciplinary models, but in the nurture and admonition of the Lord (Eph 6:4). Rather, the raising of children, which is to adapt and equip them for the future, is, simply, "to give . . . children the opportunity to encounter the God who is present, operative and revealed in Jesus Christ, to know Him and to learn to love and fear him."[22] No one, says Barth, has the opportunity to place the gospel before their children so often, in as many ways, over such a long and continuous period of time. And yet, it is not an endless time. Urgency to exercise discipline in this way is heightened when one realizes that while (pray God!) the child's life will not end, his or her youth will. "What will its content then have been? This is the question to which parents must seriously address themselves before it is too late."[23]

CONCLUSIONS

To draw the threads of my paper together, I want to return to the list of questions that I suggested ought to have been included in paragraph 31

20. Ibid.
21. Ibid.
22. Ibid., 283.
23. Ibid., 284.

of *The Saint Michael Report*. The first was this: even if children are not to be perceived to be the primary end of marriage, is the contemporary experience of the faithful a sufficient basis for saying so? Based on Barth's analysis of the relation between parents and children, it strikes me that "No" is an appropriate answer to this question. The determining factor in assessing just what the end of marriage is, is not advances in reproductive technology, nor the authority our culture gives to individuals to determine the shape of their lives through the sheer exercise of will (what I have described to my students as "voluntarism on speed"). For the freedom exercised in such choices, as far as Barth is concerned, must for the Christian always be freedom *for* obedience to the divine command of freedom exercised *alongside* others who have been covenanted to God in Christ.

Because the relation between parents and children is always authenticated and relativized by the command of God, there can be no requirement that all married couples have children (as though infertile couples are in some way deficient), or that parental relationships be exercised exclusively along the lines of biological ties. In the one family of all who have been called in Christ to be sons and daughters of God, water is thicker than blood and therefore parents are best conceived as "elders" whose task it is to witness to the God of the gospel, the God disclosed in Jesus.

So, I think we can legitimately say (and here I respectfully and a little fearfully demur from Dr. Radner's proposal) that the conceiving and raising of children is not *the* primary end of marriage. This is not to say that the biological relationship between parents and children has become theologically dispensable! Which brings me to my second question: might it not be that children, even if not the primary end of marriage, disclose truths about the nature of humanity as being in covenantal relation with God and each other that cannot simply be passed over?

To begin to frame an answer to this question, it is worth considering just why Barth begins his discussion of the relation of parents and children from the perspective of the child. "It is part of the creaturely status of man in his relationship with other men that he is conceived and born and is thus the child of a father and a mother, and that he himself in his turn can conceive and thus become the father or mother of children."[24] If from the perspective of (potential) parents, the relationship to children

---

24. Ibid., 240.

is relativized by the freedom to obey the divine command to bear fruit in other ways, from the perspective of the child, it is not. As a child, a human being stands "immediately in a special, exclusive, and lasting relationship precisely between these two persons. The relationship is not of his choosing. He cannot annul it. He cannot replace it by any other."[25]

However much the relationship of parents to children is relativized by the divine command, it is not obliterated thereby. Indeed, it cannot be, lest we lapse into at best a Manichaean and at worst a Marcionite rejection of creation, and (crucially!) the God who creates. To be human is simply to be in relationships not of our own choosing. The primary relationship, of course, is with the God who has in Christ chosen us and freed us for obedience to him. But the relationship of parents and children does indeed bear witness to the divine-human relation precisely in the aspect that, from the human perspective, it is not a chosen one.

It simply is there, never in general; always in particular. I am this body that is the product of Ellard and Kathryn Perry both biologically and as having been raised by them in the fear and admonition of the Lord. I am not a generic child in relation to a generic parent. I am Tim. As Tim, I am uniquely related to Ellard and Kathryn. I had no choice in that relation even as that relation is, whether I like it or not, constitutive of me. Thus, in the Godward aspect, parental love as a mirror of the divine love is from first to last, material. It has to do with particular bodies in particular relation.

Here I wish to raise a suspicion. It has been pointed out by my colleague, Chris Holmes, and by Professor Radner in their respective essays, that many contemporary discussions of marriage suffer from an over-sentimentalization and idealization. Dr. Radner has pointed to John Milton as an early exponent of such a view. It is a peculiarly modern notion—still resisted by some traditional cultures to today—that marriage cannot be founded on mere duty or routine or worst of all, social arrangement, but must, rather, involve the kindling of the fires of desire and romance. The deliberate inclusion of children within a theology of marriage gives the Christian the theological resources to refuse such a reduction. Children allow us to show that the love that sacramentally expressed the love of Christ for the Church is not desire over duty, but desire expressed in and through duty, in and through the daily routines of simply being a parent.

25. Ibid.

The divine love to which Christian marriage is ideally to point is not some Gnostic disembodied feeling anymore that it is the expression of some narcissistic need for self-fulfillment. It is at points all too tangible and expressed in ways and at times when personal fulfillment is the furthest thing from one's mind. I speak here as a father of a young family who has been a victim of the three "p's." That is, as someone who has been puked on, pooped on, and peed on. The language may put some of you off. I don't much mind. That—as all parents know—is the lived, material experience of parental love. A love that I cannot withhold, a love that has created a relation in which my children have had no choice. And in all that wonderful materiality, that love is, in grace, called by the triune God to be a mirror of the love of the triune God for all his children. Who has in Christ elected us before the foundation of the world.

www.ingramcontent.com/pod-product-compliance
Lightning Source LLC
Chambersburg PA
CBHW030111170426
43198CB00009B/583